Economics of Solid Waste Management in the Urban Segment of Developing Countries

Economics of Solid Waste Management in the Urban Segment of Developing Countries

R. Thiruppathi & Sathya J

ABHIJEET PUBLICATIONS
NEW DELHI 110002

ABHIJEET PUBLICATIONS
4658-A, First Floor, Ambika Bhawan,
21 Ansari Road, New Delhi 110002
Phone: 011-23259444
E-mail: abhijeetpublication@gmail.com
www.abhijeetpublications.com

ECONOMICS OF SOLID WASTE MANAGEMENT IN THE URBAN SEGMENT OF DEVELOPING COUNTRIES

First Published 2020

ISBN 978-93-88865-32-6

PRINTED IN INDIA

Published by J.K. Singh for Abhijeet Publications, New Delhi-110002, Lasertypeset by Abhijeet Typesetters, New Delhi and Printed at Dynamic Printers, New Delhi.

Preface

In olden days waste disposal did not emerge as a problem, since the population was scarce and the usage of material resource was less. The menace of waste disposal has become more serious in recent times due to rapid population growth and uncontrolled industrial growth. Solid wastes if not properly disposed or managed will not only harm humans but also impart serious threat to one's economy and environment. The solid waste management is a complex issue in developing countries like India since there exist vast variations in the types of wastes generated by different class of people from different localities such as rural, urban and semi urban. Majority of the people were unaware of the ill effects of improper disposal of solid waste. Thus the authorities in developing countries felt that it was a great challenge to them to handle this task.

In this context, the book attempts to examine the issues of municipal solid waste management in the urban segment of India, a developing country. The authors of the book conducted an empirical investigation during 2012 – 2018 to find out the ground reality in this regard.

For this purpose, the contents of the book are divided into seven chapters. The first chapter deals with the introduction and design of the study. The second chapter presents the conceptual clarification and theoretical background of the issues of solid waste management. The third chapter describes the strategies of solid waste management at the international level. The legal framework concerning the municipal solid waste management is discussed. The fourth chapter consists of the analysis relating to the quantum of solid waste generated and its disposal methods. The willingness to pay for improved solid waste management is assessed. The impact of improper solid waste management on public health is analysed in this chapter. The fifth chapter comprises the analysis pertaining to health concerns of sanitary workers. The sixth chapter analyses the challenges faced by the residents at the garbage dumping area. The seventh chapter recapitulates the summary of findings, suggestions and conclusion. This book will immensely help the scholars who are desirous in doing their research in the field of waste management.

AUTHORS

Contents

1

Introduction and Design of the Study

1.1 Introduction

In olden days waste disposal did not emerge as a problem, since the population was scarce and the usage of material resource was less. The menace of waste disposal has become more serious in recent times due to rapid population growth and uncontrolled industrial growth. Solid wastes if not properly disposed or managed will not only harm humans but also impart serious threat to one's economy and environment. The solid waste management is a complex issue in developing countries like India since there exist vast variations in the types of wastes generated by different class of people from different localities such as rural, urban and semi urban. Majority of the people were unaware of the ill effects of improper disposal of solid waste. Thus the authorities in developing countries felt that it was a great challenge to them to handle this task.

Solid waste management is one of the major functions of Municipal Corporations. It is the responsibility of the Municipal Corporation to keep the cities clean and to provide better sanitary conditions to the citizens. The sanitary conditions mean the provision of cleanliness on roads and other public places, provision of pure drinking water and provision of public toilet facilities. It is also the duty of the Municipal Corporation to collect the domestic as well as industrial garbage and to dispose them off in an appropriate manner.

Solid Waste Management is a systematic activity of collection and disposal of solid wastes. An effective management of solid waste would be to expedite and regulate the process of collection and disposal of solid wastes. The expenditure incurred on solid waste management is not an expenditure but an investment on the health care of the public. Provision for sanitation is the prime responsibility of Municipal Corporations.

Municipal solid waste includes commercial and residential wastes generated in Municipal or notified areas in either solid or semi-solid form excluding industrial and hazardous wastes but including treated bio-medical wastes.

The urban authorities in India faced a formidable challenge in the matter of municipal solid waste management due to an alarming increase in population along with huge industrial development. The prevailing strategies adopted by our urban authorities in managing solid waste were insufficient and inefficient. The lagging was observed in the matter of lack of finance and lack of technology. The authorities failed to correctly examine the socio-economic and ecological issues in solid waste management.

The generation of solid waste in India has been the serious concern and it is ever growing. In India, the states viz. Maharashtra, Tamil Nadu and Utter Pradesh were the largest generators of solid waste. In India the per capita waste generation is 377 grams and disposal is 273 grams with an average collection efficiency of 72 percent based on sample analysis done by the Central Pollution Control Board (CPCB, 2016).

Municipal Corporations and Municipalities in Tamil Nadu generate about 10870 MT of solid waste per day of which 40- 60 percent is bio-degradables, 20 – 40 percent is silt & debris and 20 percent is Recyclables. In Tamil

Nadu the per capita generation of waste varies from 0.30kg to 0.60 kg (TNPCB, 2017). The area of the present study viz. Salem Corporation generates about 400 million tones of solid waste daily (Salem Corporation Office, 2018). At present the wastes collected from 60 wards have been dumped in the dumping yard located at Chettichavadi village. Sanitary land filling and incineration are the methods adopted in the management of municipal solid wastes in the dumping yard. Organic wastes have been separated from inorganic wastes and composting was adopted as a method of managing it.

People residing in the surroundings of the garbage dumping area, are supposed to be suffered from health disorders. Thus Municipal Corporation should provide the required amenities to the people residing in the dumping areas.

Initially the wastes generated from the corporation were dumped in four places viz. Suramangalam, Veeranam, Erumapalayam and Maniyanur. A private company from Gujarat has attempted to run the solid waste management unit at Chettichavadi. It attempted to recover some recycled materials from solid waste. Due to many technical and financial constraints that operation was stopped. Thus at present the corporation has failed to adopt any scientific method of solid waste management.

Salem Corporation has proposed to locate a modern scientific solid waste management plant at 14 places. Each plant may have a capacity to manage around five to eight tones of waste generated. The plants are micro composting in nature, which will attempt to segregate and compost the organic wastes into manure.

1.2 Management of Municipal Solid Wastes

1. Any municipal solid waste generated in a city or a town, shall be managed and handled in accordance with the criteria and procedure laid down by the authority.

2. The waste processing and disposal facilities to be set up by the municipal authority on their own or through an operator of a facility shall meet the specifications and standards specified.

1.3 Sources of Municipal Solid Wastes

Municipal solid wastes could be generated from various sources. The major sources of municipal solid wastes have been enumerated as follows:

1. Residential sources such as households
2. Industrial sources such as manufacturing and chemical plants
3. Commercial sources such as shops, restaurants, hotels and offices
4. Institutional sources such as schools, colleges and hospitals
5. Construction sources like road sides, building sites etc.
6. Municipal services like landscaping, street sweeping, waste water treatment plants and
7. Agriculture sources such as orchards, crops, dairies, chicken farms, etc.

1.4 Waste Minimization

The municipal solid wastes are to be minimized by adopting either of the following methods:

1. Prevention of waste being generated is known as waste reduction which is an important method of waste management.
2. The modern concepts based on the three R's are:
   a. Reduce
   b. Reuse and
   c. Recycle

3. Avoidance of waste by using second hand goods, manufacturing goods capable of reusing and postponing the purchase of new goods by repairing them.
4. Methods of avoidance include reuse of second hand products, design products to be refillable or reusable, repair broken items instead of buying new etc.

1.5 Steps Involved in Municipal Solid Waste Management

The following steps are involved in municipal solid waste management:

- Segregation and sorting of waste at source
- Primary collection from the doorstep
- Daily street sweeping
- Storage in covered bins
- Transportation in covered vehicles
- Processing through composting/waste to energy
- Disposal of rejects/inert

1.6 Role of Sanitary Workers in Solid Waste Management

Sanitation works are assigned to the sanitary workers employed in the Municipal Corporations. They could be classified as the workers employed in cleaning, collecting and loading works. The cleaning workers start their work in the early morning. They go to every street of the area for which he/she is deputed. The particular worker has to keep the area clean by sweeping the roads and cleaning the drainage. He/she has to ensure that the waste water flows freely in the drainages. They dump the garbage after sorting the garbage into degradable and non-degradable wastes.

The sanitary workers will be supervised by the official employed in this regard. He maintains the attendance register of the sanitary workers and assigns duty to the workers. They will be deputed to specific areas and they have to cover that specific area at the stipulated time. The second type of workers will be engaged for the collection of solid waste from the huge garbage drums kept in prominent places. For this purpose, trucks and lorries are provided. The garbage so dumped in the huge drums are supposed to be dumped in an outer area and disposed off frequently.

As the domestic and industrial wastes are properly cleaned by the sanitary workers, the area becomes clean and smart. So, the fear of health issues to the public is reduced to a greater extent. The loading workers will be deputed to shift the garbage from the local garbage collection drums to the large garbage collection drums kept at public places. The best management of solid waste is to clean the city, collect and dispose the garbage in an efficient manner.

The industrial wastage is also collected and dumped at the specific places. The garbage so collected should be disposed off frequently in order to avoid health disorders of the citizens. Since the sanitary workers are engaged in the cleaning, collecting and disposing works, they are prone to health issues due to handling of garbage. Their health is one of the major concerns for the Municipal Corporations. For this purpose, they are instructed to wear overcoats, caps, uniforms and gloves.

1.7 Statement of the Problem

Solid wastes are to be properly collected and disposed properly. Otherwise, it will result in flooding and unsanitary conditions. By this worse conditions, the flies would breed in some kinds of solid wastes. They will be causing very dangerous kinds of diseases. The blocked or stagnant drainage and rain water would be the places of breeding for mosquitoes. The diseases like malaria and dengue are spread by mosquitoes. It is the responsibility of the local authority to deal with the solid waste. Salem Municipal Corporation is one of the growing corporations in the

State of Tamil Nadu. The solid waste management adopted by the Corporation becomes crucial in maintaining the health and sanitation of the citizens residing inside the corporation limits. The effective solid waste management is to be followed by the Salem Corporation in spite of the different quantity and types of solid waste disposed by the inhabitants of Salem. The Corporation authorities follow various kinds of disposal methods. In this context, the following research questions have been probed in this study:

1. How much quantum of solid wastes has been produced by the residents of Salem Corporation?
2. What are the types of solid wastes produced and disposal methods followed by the residents of Salem Corporation?
3. What kind of health issues have been faced by the sanitary workers of Salem Corporation?
4. How much the public are willing to pay for the better management of solid wastes?
5. What are the challenges faced by the residents in garbage dumping yards?
6. Whether Salem Corporation is efficient in solid waste management?

1.8 Objectives of the Study

The present study has been undertaken with the following objectives:

1. To examine the quantum of solid waste, types of solid waste and its disposal methods.
2. To analyze the health concerns of sanitary workers.
3. To measure the willingness of the public to pay for the better management of solid waste.
4. To identify the challenges faced by the residents in the garbage dumping area.

5. To assess the efficiency of Salem Corporation in solid waste management.
6. To offer suggestions for improving the municipal solid waste management.

1.9 Area of the Study

The present study attempts to examine the issues of municipal solid waste management in Salem Corporation. Salem has been declared as Salem City Municipal Corporation on 1.6.1994. The task of solid waste management has been done by sanitary inspectors and a team of sanitary supervisors and workers. Salem Corporation consists of 60 wards, categorized under four Zonal Offices, namely Suramangalam Zone, Hasthampatty Zone, Ammapet Zone, and Kondalampatty Zone. The total population of the Corporation is 913188 in March 2017. The solid wastes generated from houses, commercial establishments, roads, streets, drainages, markets, hospitals and other establishments were collected, transported and disposed in three stages viz. primary, secondary and tertiary. The Corporation disposes around 400 tones of waste of which 90–95 percent are managed (www.salemcorporation.gov.in, 2018). The Corporation has large commercial centers, residential areas and industrial activities. Huge amount of wastes have been generated from the areas like Shevapet, New bus stand, Old bus stand, VOC market and Gugai. Regarding the types of wastes generated, there exists a vast variations in its nature such as organic, inorganic, and hazardous wastes.

1.10 Research Methodology

The present study has been designed with three dimensions. In the first dimension, the study makes an attempt to quantify the solid waste produced by the households of Salem Corporation, type of solid waste produced by them and the methods of disposal followed by them. The sanitary workers dealing with the solid waste are prone to health issues while handling the solid wastes. In order to bring out the health issues of such sanitary workers another dimension of analysis has been made in this study. The third dimension of the study is related to the challenges faced by the residents, dwelling nearby the garbage dumping yard.

1.11 Data Source

The data required for the present study have been collected through primary sources i.e., the researcher has collected the relevant data from the sample respondents. The sample are of three different groups – households of Salem Corporation, sanitary workers and households at the dumping yard. The sample respondents have been selected from three groups of population and the data has been collected from the selected respondents. The secondary data have been collected from Salem Corporation Office and Pollution Control Board, Salem. The other secondary data sources include books, journals and websites.

1.12 Data Collection

The relevant data has been collected from the selected respondents of three groups using an interview schedule. For this purpose, separate interview schedules have been drafted for different groups of respondents – households of Salem Corporation, sanitary workers and households at the garbage dumping yard. The first schedule contains questions relating to the quantum of solid waste produced by the households, type of solid waste and disposal methods, while the second interview schedule comprises questions relating to the health issues of sanitary workers involved in the solid waste management and the third interview schedule is designed in such a way to collect the information relating to the challenges faced by the households at the garbage dumping yard.

1.13 Sample Size

The sample size of each group has been determined as follows:

Table 1.1: Size of the Sample

S. No.	*Name of the Groups*	*No. of Sample Respondents*
1	Households of Salem Corporation	385
2	Sanitary Workers	193
3	Households at the Dumping Yard	300

The sample size has been determined separately for each of the groups of the sample respondents by applying Cochran equation.

The formula for Cochran's equation is

$$n_0 = \frac{z^2 pq}{e^2}$$

where, e = margin error, p = proportion of the population, q = 1 − p, z value for given level of confidence.

Determination of Sample size for Households in Salem Corporation

The total number of households in Salem Corporation in four zones is 234264.

Margin Error e = 95 percent, p = 0.5, q = 0.5, z value = 1.96

$$n_0 = \frac{z^2 pq}{e^2}$$

$$n_0 = \frac{(1.96)^2 (0.5) (0.5)}{(0.05)^2}$$

$$n_0 = 385$$

Thus the sample size for households is 385.

Determination of Sample size for Sanitary Workers in Salem Corporation

Total number of sanitary workers = 1922

Margin Error e = 95 percent, p = 0.5, q=0.5, z value = 1.96

$$n_0 = \frac{z^2 pq}{e^2}$$

$$n_0 = \frac{(1.96)^2 (0.5)(0.5)}{(0.05)^2}$$

$n_0 = 385$

Since the total number of sanitary workers is small, the following formula is applied.

$$n = \frac{n_0}{1 + \frac{(n_0 - 1)}{N}}$$

$$n = \frac{385}{1 + \frac{385 - 1}{1922}}$$

n = 193

Thus the sample size for sanitary workers is 193.

Determination of Sample size for Households in Chettichavadi Village, Salem Corporation

Total number of households in Chettichavadi Village = 1350

Margin Error e = 95 percent, p = 0.5, q=0.5, z value = 1.96

$$n_0 = \frac{z^2 pq}{e^2}$$

$$n_0 = \frac{(1.96)^2 (0.5)(0.5)}{(0.05)^2}$$

$$n_0 = 385$$

Since the total number of households in Chettichavadi village is small, the following formula is applied.

$$n = \frac{n_0}{1 + \frac{(n_0 - 1)}{N}}$$

$$n = \frac{385}{1 + \frac{385 - 1}{1350}}$$

$$n = 300$$

Thus the sample size for sanitary workers is 300.

1.14 Sampling Method

The sample of the first population viz. households of Salem Corporation has been selected using stratified random sampling method. The Salem Corporation has been divided into four zones (strata) and the total sample households of 385 have been selected from four zones in proportion to its total number of households in each zone as detailed in the following table.

Table 1.2: Sampling Methodology

Zones	*Total Number of Households*	*Sample size*
Suramangalam	67538	111
Hasthampatty	53553	88
Ammapet	63275	104
Kondalampatty	49898	82
Total	**234264**	**385**

Source: Salem Corporation, 2018.

The sample respondents of the second population viz. sanitary workers have been selected on the basis of systematic random sampling. In this regard, the list of sanitary workers has been obtained from the Salem Municipal Corporation and the respondents have been selected using systematic random sampling method.

The samples of the third population viz. households at the garbage dumping area have been selected by adopting simple random sampling.

1.15 Hypotheses

1. The socio economic status of the respondents plays a major role in determining the quantum of solid waste generated by them.
2. The health conditions of the public depends upon the efficiency of waste management in their locality.
3. The amount of willingness to pay for the management of solid waste is the function of variables viz. income, education, quantity of solid waste generated and types of solid waste generated.
4. Methods of disposal and the management of solid waste is similar in all the zones of corporation.
5. The health conditions of the sanitary workers depend upon the nature of sanitary work in which they are involved.
6. The provision and usage sanitary materials play a major role in safeguarding the health of the sanitary workers.

7. The residents living in the nearby areas of the dumping yard are affected more by health issues rather than residents living in faraway places.
8. The awareness about the effects of garbage dumping depends upon the socio economic status of the residents.

1.16 Statistical Tools Used

The data obtained from the sample respondents viz. households of Salem Corporation, sanitary workers and households at garbage dumping areas have been put through analysis by applying the appropriate statistical tools as enlisted below:

1. Percentage analysis
2. Mean
3. Standard Deviation
4. ANOVA (Analysis of Variance)
5. Multiple Regression
6. Binary Logit Regression and
7. Chi Square test

1.17 Limitations of the Study

The research studies are subject to certain limitations. The present study also has the following limitations:

1. Since the study is mainly based on the primary data, the choices of respondents could be biased even though care has been taken for avoiding the bias.
2. The choices of respondents would vary from time to time and place to place. Hence, care has to be taken while generalizing the results of the study to other similar areas.
3. The study has covered only household waste and not the commercial and industrial wastes for the analysis of primary data.
4. The size of sample has been confined to 385 for the households of Salem Corporation, 193 for

sanitary workers and 300 for households at the garbage dumping area.

1.18 Chapter Scheme

The thesis has been organized with seven chapters as described below:

The first chapter deals with the introduction and design of the study. It includes the introduction of solid waste management, statement of the problem, objectives of the study, research methodology and limitations of the study.

The second chapter has been divided into three parts dealing with the conceptual clarification, theoretical framework and review of past studies related to the present study.

The third chapter describes the strategies of solid waste management at the international level, national level, state level and the study area. The legal framework concerning the municipal solid waste management is discussed.

The fourth chapter consists of the analysis relating to the quantum of solid waste generated and its disposal methods in Salem Corporation. The willingness to pay for improved solid waste management is assessed. The impact of improper solid waste management on public health is analysed in this chapter. The efficiency of Salem Corporation in municipal solid waste management is assessed.

The fifth chapter comprises the analysis pertaining to health concerns of sanitary workers.

The sixth chapter analyses the challenges faced by the residents at the garbage dumping area viz. Chettichavadi.

The seventh chapter recapitulates the summary of findings, suggestions and conclusion of the study.

2

Concepts, Theoretical Framework and Review of Literature

The review of the existing literature related to the study is quite essential to have as insight into the concrete framework of the study. At the same time, it is essential to understand the concepts and theoretical framework of the study which will be helpful to design and carry out the study smoothly. This chapter has been divided into two parts. The first part of this chapter presents the concepts and theoretical framework of the study while the second part consists of an overview of the previous literature.

2.1 Conceptual Framework of the Study

Solid Waste Management has been the prime focus of the present study. However, there are many other related terms which are to be understood necessarily in framing the theme of the study. The related concepts include the source, origin and type of solid waste and its disposal methods.

Types of Solid Waste

The following are the major types of solid waste defined in New Solid Waste Management Rules 2016. Depending on its source and origin it is classified into different types.

Domestic / Residential Waste

This category of domestic waste is originated from the day to day activities of households such as cleaning, cooking, repairing, packaging, clothing, writings and old furnishings. Households also discard bulky wastes such as furniture and large appliances which cannot be repaired and used.

Municipal Waste

Municipal solid waste includes commercial and household wastes excluding industrial hazardous waste but including treated bio-medical wastes. It is in the form of either solid or semi solid generated within the limits of municipal or notified area is defined as municipal solid waste.

Commercial Waste

This category of solid waste originates from commercial and trade centres such as wholesale and retail shops, hotels, offices, markets, warehouses etc. The commercial wastes can be categorized into garbage and rubbish.

Institutional Waste

Institutional wastes refer to waste arising from institutions such as schools, colleges, hospitals and research institutes. This type waste can be classified into three categories such as garbage, rubbish and hazardous wastes. It includes wastes which are classified as garbage and rubbish as well as wastes which are considered to be hazardous to public health and to the environment.

Garbage

Garbage includes animal and vegetable wastes resulting from its handling, storing, sale, preparation, cooking and serving. Garbage emits strong odour. Since it contains purtrecible organic matter it attracts rats, files and other vermin. Thus its storage, processing and disposal should be properly done to avoid its negative effects.

Rubbish

Rubbish refers to the type of solid waste originates from household, commercial and institutional activities. It excludes garbage and ashes.

Ashes

Ashes are the residues of burning of wood, charcoal, coal and other combustible materials used for cooking in houses, institutions and small industrial establishments. If it is produced in large quantities at power plants and factories it will be categorized in to industrial wastes.

Bulky Wastes

Bulky wastes refer to the wastes generated in households which cannot be stored in normal containers. This includes worn out household appliances. This category of wastes will be largely disposed by developed countries due to their pattern of consumption. The metallic types of bulky wastes can be recyclable and the remaining should be discarded.

Street Sweeping

This category of waste were collected from street sweeping, which is the major mode of waste collection followed in developing countries, where the wastes were littered in streets. This type of waste contains both garbage and rubbish.

Dead Animals

Dead animals refer to the animals died by either naturally or accidently. The wastes discarded from slaughter houses will not come under this category. For the purpose of handling, dead animals have been classified into small and large animals. This type of waste has to be handled and managed properly which will be harmful otherwise.

Construction and Demolition Wastes

The waste discarded from construction and demolition sites such as earth, concrete, wires, plumping materials, bricks and stones will be categorized under construction and demolished wastes.

Industrial Wastes

This category of waste was discarded in the manufacturing and industrial activities. The industrial wastes disposed will be different depending on the nature of industrial activity.

Hazardous Wastes

Waste which are potentially hazardous to human beings and environment due to its chemical, biological and physical properties will be classified as hazardous wastes. This may be disposed by various activities viz. industrial, institutional and commercial origin.

Sewage Wastes

The solid waste which are the bye products of sewage treatment were categorized as sewage wastes. Mostly it is organic in its nature originated from raw and treated sewage. Sludge and grit were the major categories of solids found in raw and treated sewage.

Methods of Solid Waste Management

As per the New Solid Waste Management Rules, 2016, which are the regulatory framework governing municipal solid waste management, the following are the definitions for various methods of Solid Waste Management.

Collection

It refers to the process of collecting waste from various

sources. It also refers to the collection of waste from bins and shifting to secondary location points.

Segregation

It is the method of sorting and separating waste into different categories based on its nature as bio degradable, non bio degradable and hazardous wastes.

Processing

It refers to the activity of transforming the nature of solid waste into manageable form.

Recycling

It refers to the conversion of solid waste into valuable resources which can be utilized in the production of new goods. The recycled product may or may not be in the same quality to the original products.

Storage

Storage of waste means temporary storing of wastes in safe manner to avoid its littering, attraction of files and stray animals and emission of odour.

Transportation

It refers to the method of conveyance of municipal solid waste from one place to another in a hygienic manner with the scientifically designed vehicles to avoid odour and littering.

Composting

It is a controlled process of microbial decomposition of organic matter present in the solid wastes.

Disposal

It is the final disposal of municipal solid wastes as per the specified norms and measures to prevent contamination of ground water, surface water and ambient air quality.

Bio-Methanation

It is a process, which enables the enzymatic decomposition of the organic matter present in the municipal solid waste by microbial action to produce methane rich biogas.

Land Filling

It is a method of disposal of solid wastes on land with a facility of protection to avoid contamination of ground and surface water, littering of waste, air pollution, attraction of birds, flies and rodents and soil pollution.

Leachate

It is in the form of liquid seeping through solid wastes and other mediums, which has the extracts of dissolved or suspended elements from the solid waste.

Vermicomposting

Vermicomposting is a process of using earthworms to convert the biodegradable wastes into compost.

2.2 Theoretical Framework of the Study

The present study is based on the theory of externality to analyze the negative externality posed by the improper management of solid waste. The impact of pollution caused by improper disposal and management of solid waste on human health was the aim of the study, which was carried out on the basis of theory of externality.

Theory of Externality

Externality refers to the actions of persons or firms affecting other's entity without permission. Externality may be positive or negative. Negative externalities are referred as external costs and positive externalities as external benefits. There is a good wealth of literature concerning the economic and political analysis of theory of externality including the studies of Pigou, Baumol, Oates and Ronald Coase. The authors have suggested for the intervention of Government and recognition of property rights to overcome the problem of negative externalities.

Roland Coase (1960) suggested the inclusion of property rights to tackle the problem of inefficiency caused by externality. To tackle negative externality such as pollution, Coase has suggested to award property right to the polluter, and the victims of pollution should have to offer to pay to make the polluter to reduce their output. In case of positive externality such as for clean air/water, the property right should be awarded to victim and the polluter has to offer to pay the victim.

Thomas D. Crocker and Alan Randall (1976) Baumol and Oates have dealt with the issues of marginal social cost and the determination of social optimum output. They have advocated a two stage approach to solve the problem of externality and attaining social optimum. The first stage involves the determination of ambient standard based on available social knowledge and social preference. The second stage is the determination of charges based on standards and the marginal abatement cost.

Ng and Yang (1993) the authors attempted to analyse the allocation and organizational effects of externalities with the help of inframarginal analysis of externalities. The authors suggested that taxes should be imposed on those sectors that generate negative externality and subsidy should be given to the sectors that suffer from the negative externality.

Charles D. Kolstad (1996) has discussed about negative externality in the form of pollution, which slowly accumulates over time causing huge damage. He pointed out that the key feature of environmental economics was the presence of high degree of externality. Since there was a problem of asymmetrical information and uncertainty about the occurrence of environmental problems, it was needed to have perfect knowledge to take perfect decisions.

Barnett. H and Bruce Yandle (1999) in their paper traced the history of the theory of externality. Pigou has given political solutions to the problems of externalities. Pigou has suggested for the Government intervention to solve the problem of externality, since the divergence between private and social net product cannot be solved through private contractual arrangements. Coase, in contrast to Pigou, has suggested for the inclusion of property rights to minimize externalities. Later on Pigou modified his argument stating that externalities could be solved by enhancing market operations.

Brain P. Simpson (2007) in his paper has discussed about the economic, political and philosophical dimensions of externalities. The recipient of the externality was no way connected with cost and benefit bestowed upon him. There is a market failure in case of externalities. Thus the negative externality is failed to be reflected in the market price. The government intervention in the form of stringent actions through legislative and fiscal measures was the only solution to minimize the negative externalities.

The theory of externality is applied in identifying both the negative and positive externalities associated with the municipal solid waste management in the study area.

2.3 Review of Past Studies

This part of the chapter discusses the published source of information by different scholars and researchers. The review of past studies were useful in analyzing the present study in new dimensions and to give new interpretations.

Past Studies Related to Waste Management and Its Impact on Environment

Medina M, (1997), in her paper analysed the relationship between waste generation and income by involving 123 countries based on the data compiled by the United Nations.

Her study found that for the wealthiest countries the association between waste generation and income was weak. The model used in the study indicates that when the country develops its generation of waste increases.

Shuchi Gupta, et. al, (1998), have observed that the management of solid waste in India was chaotic and unscientific. The uncontrolled dumping of wastes at the outskirts of cities without proper management was found to cause serious environmental degradation in the form of ground water pollution. The authors have suggested the need for policy and guidelines to enable the municipal bodies to enable better management of solid waste.

Ravichandran et. al, (1999), in their article have attempted to analyse the magnitude of the problem of solid waste management in Tiruchirappalli Corporation. The methodologies adopted for waste management were assessed in the paper. The higher growth of population was found to be a major factor affecting the efficiency in the management of solid waste.

Mansoor Alam Siddique, (2000), has found that urbanization resulted in the menaces viz. uncontrolled growth of solid, liquid and gaseous waste. The author has suggested for the inclusion of stakeholders viz. villages and NGOs in enabling the proper management of solid waste.

Bhide, (2001), has found that the major determinant of waste generation in urban area was the growth of population and industrialization.

Gopalakrishnan, (2001), in his article has analyzed that proper management of solid waste require a proper planning regarding the size and number of receptacles, size and number of collection cars and number of workers required for collection.

Kim Peters, (2001), the study in Naorobi reveals that in low-income areas, poor people were occupied in rag picking as a means of their livelihood. These people do not usually scavenge organic waste but street children often pick through bins to find their next meals. In these low-income areas, organic components comprise about ninety percent of the total waste and toxic material is estimated to about 0.2 percent of the total waste. Urban farmers station their livestock near waste heaps where the animals can feed on the disposed waste. In feeding directly on waste, animals can be injured by sharp or poisonous objects. In warm climate, pathogen growth in kitchen waste occurs rapidly and livestock become infected. He concludes that the role played by NGO's, CBO's and local authorities is essential to deal with the environmental problems and poverty.

Roy et al., (2001), the authors have reported that among rag pickers handling and sorting of recyclable materials from waste bins the containing toxic wastes causes diseases like worm infestations. Viral hepatitis, gastroenteritis, skin diseases and a number of deadly diseases being carried through needle and infected blood. Even qualified doctors are not sure whether the needles and syringes being used by them are recycled or genuine ones. Disposal syringes and needle, which should be junked after one use, are in wide circulations.

Syed Mahmoor Anwar, (2001), in his study attempted to analyse the practices of households in disposing their solid waste in Dhaka city. It was found that majority of households threw their waste in improper way into roadsides, canals and sewage channels.

Singhal et al., (2001), have found that the growth in municipal solid waste in urban centers has outpaced the population growth in recent years and tend to increase the demand for land for disposing of waste. The integration of private sector, non-government organizations and rag pickers was suggested to achieve efficient management of solid waste.

Christine Furedy, (2002) has analysed the efficacy of various methods of waste management and found that controlled composting was the safest method. The revenue generated from compost plants in developing countries were found insignifi,ant. The composing plants installed at developing countries were failed to survive for long years.

Chabra, (2003), in his paper has discussed the various options for the management of solid waste. Anaerobic Digestion was found to be the efficient one in managing the solid waste.

Koushki, (2004), in his study examined the efficiency of municipal solid waste management in Kuwait. The solid waste management in Kuwait was compared with the waste management in other countries. The low lobour and energy cost were mainly responsible for the favorable cost of management, collection and transportation of residential waste in Kuwait.

Jain, (2005), it was found that 80 percent of total Municipal Solid Waste generated in Indian cities contains bio degradable materials. The waste collection and management in Indian cities was found inadequate and unscientific. The major constraints of the municipal solid waste management faced in Indian cities were discussed.

Almithra H. Patel, (2006), has suggested for the sanitization of solid waste in order to avoid odours, smoke, fire and leachate. Sprinkling of water mixed with cow dung and rock phosphate powder was suggested as the method of sanitization on fresh waste.

Kannal Achuthan, (2007), in his article stressed the need for privatization of III zone of Chennai Corporation. The author suggested the source segregation and composting as the method of solid waste management to avoid mere dumping of solid wastes at dump sities.

Raman N and D Sathiya Narayanan (2008), attempted to analyse the impact of dumping of solid waste on soil and ground water near Pallavaram land filling site, Chennai. The physical and chemical parameters of soil and ground water samples collected near the land filling site was examined. It was found that the ground water sources were contaminated due to the dumping of solid waste.

Suda Goel (2008), has revealed that the solid waste management was the most neglected environmental problem in India. The major problems faced in Indian cities in the matter of solid waste management were underestimation of waste generation and resource requirement for its management and lack of reliable data and information in the field of waste management.

Thanh N P et al., (2010) in their study attempted to evaluate the quantity and composition of household waste generated in Can Tho city in Southern Vietnam with a sample of 100 households. The aim of the study was to identify the scope of recycling of household waste. The study has found that there was a positive correlation between per capita waste generation and level of urbanization and population density. The authors calculated that the green house gas emission was 292.25 gm per capita per day from the biodegradable components of household waste per capita per day.

Anne Scheinberg et al., (2010) in their article based on the "Third World Report on Water and Sanitation in World Cities" revealed that the major constraint observed in the solid waste management systems among world cities was the lack of consistent and strict global standards for solid waste management and recycling.

Noorjahan Arif & M. Ravichandran (2011) in their book discussed the behavior of selected households in managing their solid waste in Tiuchirappalli Corporation, Tamil Nadu. The institutional measures undertaken by the municipal corporation in collecting, transporting and disposing the solid waste were elaborated in the book. The occupational health hazards faced by conservancy workers were analysed. The authors examined the scope of clean development mechanism by reducing methane emission through the proper management of solid wastes.

Nadi Behzad, (2011) , the solid waste management was the major issue addressed by the Malaysian

Government due to rise in population and arrival of tourists, economic growth, inadequate enforcement of waste legislation, poor infrastructure and public attitudes towards waste disposal. The paper aimed to discuss the state of waste management practices and problems in Malaysia.

Ojok et al., (2012), in their study attempted to evaluate the willingness to pay for better municipal solid waste management by households at a place Kampala in Uganda. The willingness to pay has been measured with the tool of contingent valuation. The study has found that the factors viz. gender, age, family size, educational level, income level, marital status and migration status were significantly associated with the amount of willingness to pay for improved solid waste management.

Bhatt M S and Asheref Illiyan (2012), in their book have mentioned that in Indian scenario solid waste management was a multidimensional and challenging task. In India municipal solid waste has been increasing in alarming proportions, but the public agencies were not found to tackle the menace with its rising magnitude. The higher economic growth was also responsible to make the issue of solid waste management a more complex one. The generation of reliable information and awareness about the impacts of solid waste were the need of the hour.

Chandrappa, Ramesha et al., (2012) , the problem of solid waste have started to emerge even before the problems of water and air pollution attracted public attention. The characteristics of waste have been ever changing, due to the changes in culture, geography and income at world countries. Due to the transition of world economies over a period of time there has been as explosion of waste. The approaches of solid waste management would not be the same in all the countries. It is not only the role of local bodies to tackle the problem of solid waste in every country. The authors have suggested to incorporating the role of engineers, doctors, economists and environmentalists to deal with the problem of waste management.

Rajnarayan R. Tiwari, (2012), in his paper analysed the occupational health hazards faced by sewage and sanitary workers. It was found that sanitary workers were exposed to wide range of diseases viz. cardiovascular degeneration, musculoskeletal disorders like osteoarthritic changes and intervertebral disc hernition, infections like hepatitis, leptospirosis and helicobacter, skin problems, respiratory system problems and altered pulmonary function parameters due to their exposure to harmful gases like methane and hydrogen sulphide. He has suggested to conduct regular awareness programs to impart knowledge about safety work procedures and usage of sanitary materials.

Mohd Dinie Muhaimin Samsudina, Mashitah Mat Don, (2012), it was found that there was an increase in the generation of municipal solid wastes (MSW) in Malaysia. However, MSW management in Malaysia can be considered relatively poor and disorganized. The most preferred of MSW disposal method in Malaysia is through land filling due to several factors. This method is not sustainable and brings lot of problems. The characteristic of Malaysian MSW, reports the current practices of MSW management, and provides some suggestions to improve MSW management system in Malaysia.

Sadia Afroz Mukti, (2013), has analyzed the problems and prospects of solid waste management in Dhaka city and the trends of urban waste creation in Bangladesh. He found that the solid waste management was inefficient due to inadequate services, inadequate financing, inadequate environmental controls, poor institutional structure, inadequate understanding of complex systems, inadequate sanitation and lack of implementation of proper environmental laws. He has suggested that there should be an integrated system combining different methods of solid waste management

Pervez Alam (2013), has found that the vulnerable groups exposed to ill effects of solid waste were children, waste workers and population living nearby dumping of wastes. The health ailments due to impacts of solid waste were low birth weight, nausea and vomiting, chemical poisoning and congenital malformations. The preventive measures suggested were recycling and reusing of waste, waste minimization, sorting of waste, proper legislative framework concerning waste management and safe collection and handling of hazardous waste.

Syeda Maria Ali and Azra Yasmin, (2014), have found that the water quality and vegetation cover had been deteriorated due to open dumping of wastes in disposal sites. By analysing the surface sample collections of 12 from the dumping areas in Islamabad City, the authors have found the significant modifications in the soil properties at sites.

Subramani et al., (2014) in their study have attempted to identify and investigate all dump sites in Salem Corporation. From their investigation they found that the dumping sites in Salem Corporation needed immediate attention due to its severe impact on its surrounding environment.

Surindra Suthar and Pavithra Singh (2015), revealed that the composition of household waste played a significant role in deciding the municipal solid waste management plan in urban cities. The authors attempted to study the quantity and quality of waste generated by households in Dehradun city, India by using the sample of 144 households. They found that the types of solid waste generated depended upon the socio economics conditions of the households. The significant positive correlation was found between size of family and quantity of waste generated. It was concluded there was a ample scope for energy recovery from household waste, if it was properly managed.

Isaac Bright Addo and Emmanuel OPoku Acheampong, (2015), have attempted to identify the solid waste disposal methods by households and their perception about the impact of improper management of waste on public health by involving a sample of 256 households at Kumasi Metropolis, Ghana. The poor management of waste was found to cause ailments viz. chest pain, diarrhoea, intestinal worms, typhoid fever and cancer among the household members. The study recommended for the separation and reuse of wastes, sensitisation and community participation in sanitization improvement programmes.

Selvamani R and D. Rajan, (2015), in their study examined the socio economic conditions of *dalit* women sanitary workers in Tiruppur Municipal Corporation by involving 154 dalit women sanitary workers out of 257 in the study area. They found that the majority were illiterates, early married, having no saving habits and toilet facilities. A significant difference was found between education and socio economic status of sample workers. The primary and secondary methods of the social work were suggested to improve the quality of life of the *dalit* women sanitary workers.

Asare W et al., (2015) in their article attempted to assess households' solid waste generation and disposal at three places viz. Ejisu, Kwamo and Fumesua at Ghana. It was found that the place called Ejisu was the highest waste generator followed by Kwamo and Fumesua. The socio economic factors viz. income, education and size of family were found significant in determining the quantity and composition of waste generated by households. The study has suggested implementing the integrated municipal solid waste management.

Sukanya Rangamani et al., (2015), in their study attempted to examine the nature of health problems of sanitary workers using a lay epidemiological process. It was used to identify occupational health problems and deficiencies in healthcare access through the narrative of workers' perception of their illnesses. The study has found that injuries and chest pain were the commonly reported illnesses. Regarding the method of treatment, self medication was found to be common. Intake of alcohol was largely found among the sanitary workers. The non-availability of health and safety mechanisms at workplace was found.

Russell Kabir and Felicia Babs Shomoye, (2016), attempted to evaluate the health impact of residents nearby Olusosun dumpsite at Nigeria. A sample of 100 households had been included within 250 metres radius and 100 households between 250 to 500 metres radius. The study revealed that the majority of respondents were affected by health issues due to dumping of wastes in their area. It was also found that closer to the dumping area, more will be the health damage. The authors recommended that proper education and awareness should be given to residents in safeguarding their health.

Shaoli De and Biswajit Debnath, (2016), in their study have explored the adverse health of residents living in the garbage disposal area of Kolkatta viz. Garia. They found that the failure of appropriate facilities, huge amount of waste generation, inadequate space and practice of open dumping had posed severe threat to the surrounding environment and health of the public. The major health problems found were allergy, asthma, skin irritation and gastro intestinal diseases.

Pham Thi Thuy Trang et al., (2016), in their paper analyzed the households' willingness to pay for better management of waste in Thu Dau Mot city. The contingent valuation method was applied to measure the willingness to pay by including the sample of 330 households. The authors have applied logistic regression to find out the factors influencing households' willingness to pay for better solid waste management. From the logit regression it was found that higher income and more educated households were willing to pay for improved solid waste management.

Qingbin Song et al., (2016), have studied the residents' attitude towards waste management and willingness to pay for better solid waste management in Macau. By applying logistic regression they found that education was the only factor significantly associated with the willingness to pay. The other explanatory variables used in the model were age, gender, family size and income which were insignificant in determining the willingness to pay for improved waste management.

Science Daily, (2016), in an article published in the Science daily it was given that the researchers in Italy evaluated the health damages of public living near the nine different dumping sites in the Lazio region. The researchers have found the strong association between hydrogen sulphide, a major pollutant emitted from landfills and the deaths and hospitalization due to lung cancer and respiratory illnesses. The children were found to be more affected by illnesses due to the pollution emitted from landfills.

Muhdin Muhammedhussen Batu et al., (2016), in their paper attempted to find out the factors influencing the households' willingness to pay for better and improved solid waste management in Jimma Town in Ethiopia. The sample decided for the present study was 200 households. The authors have found out that the households' willingness to pay for improved solid waste management is significantly associated with the factors viz. income, possession of house and quantity of waste generated by them.

Amina Zia et al., (2017), in their study attempted to analyse and compare the quantity and composition of municipal solid waste at three socio – economic levels of respondents at four seasons by involving 1260 sample respondents. By using ANOVA statistical analysis, they found that the higher income group generated the highest amount of waste and the waste generation was huge in the seasons of spring and winter when compared to other two seasons.

Yogita V. Masur and Renuka S. Salunke , (2017), the waste disposal methods by the residents of Dharwad City have been analyzed in this paper. The role of solid waste management is significant in maintaining sanitary and hygiene life of the residents. The present study was taken to collect the primary data on waste disposal practices by the residents of various types of dwellings. All the zones from Dharwad city were selected under the study. Based on purposive sampling technique four types of dwelling namely independent, apartment, urban slum and quarters were considered. The total sample for the study comprised 390 households.

Sunil Kumar et al., (2017), in their paper has suggested the utilization of modern scientific waste management systems than relying on the waste dumps with no environmental protection. Their paper has observed the potentiality for recovering energy from landfill via methane extraction. The shortage of skilled engineers and environmental specialists was felt as the major setback in India.

Igwe Kelechi Chima and Mgbasinonwu Vincent Nwabinye., (2017), examined the household waste generation, disposal and management within Umuahia Capital Territory of Abia State, Nigeria. A sample of 100 households at 10 locations has been selected as the sample. It was found that the income and education were positively significant at 1 percent level in determining the quantity of waste and the household size negatively significant at 1 percent level.

Priyanka V. Patil and R K Kamble., (2017), in their study have analysed the occupational health hazards of sanitary workers in Chandrapur Municipal Corporation by involving a sample of 20 workers. The study revealed that the sanitary workers were exposed to wide range of environmental and occupational health hazards viz. cardiovascular degeneration, musculoskeletal disorders, headache, gastrointestinal and leptospirosis. The study has suggested that reduction in exposure and use of personal protective equipments should be encouraged.

Sherrin Sophia N and S Pavithra., (2017), in their study analysed the socio economic conditions of sanitary workers in Sengulam Colony at Tiruchirappalli by involving a sample of 60 workers. They have found that harassment by supervisors and discrimination were the major social issues faced by them. The major health issues affecting sanitary workers were gastrointestinal diseases, orthopaedic, skin and respiratory problems. They have suggested that the provision of special medical camps, safety measures and strong welfare schemes for the betterment of sanitary workers.

Shilpa P Chowti et al., (2018), have studied the health problems faced by the households residing near the dumping area at Hubballi – Dharwad Municipal Corporation and Bruhat Bengaluru Mahanagara Palike by involving the sample of 60 selected respondents. The study has found that the major health problems faced by the respondents were asthma, malaria, nose and eye irritation, respiratory problems and frequent vomiting. The authors concluded that open dumping followed in the dumping area was the major reason attributing threat to public health and environment.

Ezekiel N. Ndunda and Virgina K. Muia., (2018), in their study aimed to find out the factors influencing households' willingness to pay for better management of wastes in Nairobi, Kenya by involving the sample of 114 households residing around the dumping site in Nairobi. They have found that willingness to pay was significantly related to income, gender, family size and education. There was a positive significant relationship between income, family size and educational level and willingness to pay. The gender was found to be negatively associated with the willingness to pay.

Ramachandra T V et.al, (2018) their study has found that the per capita waste generation was positively correlated with the education and income of the households and negatively related with the size of the family in Bangalore City. The organic fraction of the total waste of the city was about 82 percent having the strong potential for recovering energy from waste. The authors have suggested the integrated solid waste management strategy to improve the efficiency in waste management through technology and policy interventions.

Critical Comments

This chapter incorporates discussions on the theoretical background, concepts and review of related works. Various concepts pertaining to sources, types and treatment of solid wastes were given. Theoretical background of the study in relation to the theory of externality is reviewed, which helps in identifying the externalities found in the management of solid waste. Large number of Indian and Foreign studies discussing the methods of solid waste management over a period of time was reviewed. The studies concerning occupational health hazards of sanitary workers and health issues of residents living near the waste dumping sites were also reviewed. The review of the studies discussing the willingness to pay at the public for improved waste management helps to identify the variables determining the willingness to pay in the present study. From the review of past studies, it was observed that during the earlier period the menace of solid waste was the most neglected environmental problem, when compared other environmental issues like air and water pollution. Only in the recent times, due to the flooding of wastes caused by urbanization, consumerism and higher population growth, the solid waste management has become the serious issue. Studies concentrating on all the aspects of solid waste management by linking the analyses of Corporation, households, sanitary workers and residents at dumping sites were inadequate, which was covered in the present study.

3

An Overview of Municipal Solid Waste and Its Management

Solid waste management and sanitation have been the prime focus of every country in the world. They are the determinants of wellness of the citizens and help to create a healthy society. The policies of the Government regarding solid waste management and urban sanitation depend highly upon the innovative service delivery models. Having realized the importance of solid waste management, the Central Government has introduced the 'Swachh Bharat' policy. Accordingly, the state governments and local authorities have been directed towards making 'Clean India'. Similarly the developing countries as well as the developed countries have been taking various initiatives to maintain the cleanliness of the nation. In this chapter, various measures taken towards solid waste management have been discussed at the international level, national level, state level and the study area.

3.1 Solid Waste Management: Universal Scenario

In this section, the solid waste generated by various countries have been described. For this purpose, the solid waste generated has been classified as food waste, paper / cardboard, wood, textiles, rubber / leather, metal, glass and other wastes. The countries have been categorized into five regions such as Asia, Africa, Europe, Oceania and America. The region's specific data relating to solid

Table 3.1 : Region-Specific Amounts of Solid Waste Generation

(in percentage)

Region	*Food Waste*	*Paper/ Cardboard*	*Wood*	*Textiles*	*Rubber/ Leather*	*Plastic*	*Metal*	*Glass*	*Others*	*Total*
Asia										
Eastern Asia	26.2	18.8	3.5	3.5	1	14.3	2.7	3.1	26.9	100
South-Central Asia	40.3	11.3	7.9	2.5	0.8	6.4	3.8	3.5	23.5	100
South-Eastern Asia	43.5	12.9	9.9	2.7	0.9	7.2	3.3	4	15.6	100
Western Asia & Middle East	41.1	18	9.8	2.9	0.6	6.3	1.3	2.2	17.8	100
Africa										
Eastern Africa	53.9	7.7	7	1.7	1.1	5.5	1.8	2.3	19	100
Middle Africa	43.4	16.8	6.5	2.5	2.7	4.5	3.5	2	18.1	100
Northern Africa	51.1	16.5	2	2.5	1.6	4.5	3.5	2	16.3	100
Southern Africa	23	25	15	1.2	1.4	3.7	2.3	2.1	26.3	100
Western Africa	40.4	9.8	4.4	1	2.3	3	1	2.4	35.7	100
Europe										
Eastern	30.1	21.8	7.5	4.7	1.4	6.2	3.6	10	14.7	100
Northern	23.8	30.6	10	2	1.2	13	7	8	4.4	100
Southern	36.9	17	10.6	5.2	1.7	12.3	2.9	1.7	11.7	100
Western	24.2	27.5	11	4.2	1.6	11.7	2.4	1.5	15.9	100
Oceania										
Australia & New Zealand	36	30	24	2	3	2	1	1	1	100
Rest of Oceania	67.5	6	2.5	2	2.4	2.1	3.1	2.7	11.7	100
America										
North America	33.9	23.2	6.2	3.9	1.4	8.5	4.6	6.5	11.8	100
Central America	43.8	13.7	13.5	2.6	1.8	6.7	2.6	3.7	11.6	100
South America	44.9	17.1	4.7	2.6	0.7	10.8	2.9	3.3	13	100
Caribbean	46.9	17	2.4	5.1	1.9	9.9	5	5.7	6.1	100

Source: Urban Development Series – Knowledge Papers, 2016**3.2** Solid Waste Management Practices at Selected World Countries

waste generated have been calculated in percent of total solid waste generated for each type of solid waste. The compositions of data include only the domestic solid waste and does not include the industrial solid waste generated in this analysis. From the analysis it can be inferred that food waste was largely discharged by less developed African countries, when compared to developed countries. The developed regions comprising American and European countries comparatively discharge more amount of plastic and paper waste, when compared to developing regions.

Solid Waste Management in China

It is well known that China is the most populous country in the world. The rapid growth of population in China forced to increase the production and consumption of goods. As a result, municipal solid waste generated in the cities of China has witnessed an unprecedented growth. Despite the steps taken by China to handle the municipal solid waste in a proper way, Persistent Organic Pollutants (POP) have caused many adverse effects in the country. In 2004, China has introduced a specialized programme to manage the municipal solid wastes viz. National Implementation Programme. Health disorders like cancer, handicap by birth, reproductive system dysfunction, poor intelligence, etc. have been suspected to be caused by the accumulated municipal solid wastes. The growth rate of municipal solid waste generated in China is found to be similar to the growth rate of its population.

Ministry of Housing, Urban and Rural Development have been responsible for the municipal solid waste management. It undertakes the municipal waste collection and disposal at the national level while the collection, transportation and disposal of solid waste at the municipal levels have been vested in the hands of Urban Management Bureaus. Standards for discharge / emissions of water pollutants, air pollutants, etc. have been issued by the Ministry of Environmental Protection.

Kumming and Ningbo have been the two major demonstration cities of environment in China. Kumming wants to come out of the traditional methods of solid waste management and has been taking various initiatives to introduce modern methods of municipal solid waste management. Accordingly, Kumming has established four incinerators with fluidized bed technology and mass burning technology. Ningbo has established three incinerators with the financial assistance from the World Bank.

Solid Waste Management in Japan

In Japan due to a rapid increase in the amount of waste, it became difficult to prevent combustible waste from being land filled without being incinerated. This resulted in an increase in the amount of waste delivered to landfills, thereby reducing the residual capacity and time of existing landfills. As Japans land mass is limited, land filling sites were difficult to be found.

0Also, mainly due to the difficulty in obtaining the agreement of residents regarding the construction of new landfills, there was a shortage of landfills especially in large cities. This made it more important than ever to reduce the amount of land filled waste. 0

One of the factors that made it difficult to construct new landfills was the opposition movements organized by residents who were concerned about the environmental pollution caused by landfills.

Thus incineration of waste was the method largely followed in Japan for its waste management. Japan possessed the world's leading garbage incineration facilities involving technologies like stoker furnaces, fluidized bed furnaces and gasification fusion resource furnaces.

The Waste Management Act placed the responsibility for industrial waste management on waste-generating business operators. However, there were business operators who lacked the sense of responsibility for covering the appropriate costs required for waste management. Such business operators outsourced waste management to waste treatment operators who were willing to undertake the management of the waste at low prices without checking whether they could properly process the waste. As a result, illegal waste dumping and other unlawful operations were undertaken by many unethical or unauthorized operators for making excessive profits, causing serious environmental pollution. Restoring contaminated soil and surrounding environments required large amounts of funds.

Also, illegal dumping of industrial waste and other unlawful operations were greatly affected by large-scale illegal dumping. There was even a case where a single dumping produced an amount of illegally discarded waste equivalent to the usual amount illegally discarded in one year. Such cases of large-scale illegal dumping highlighted the need to prevent illegal waste dumping and to stop the spread of unlawful practices.

Under the recycling policy, Japan is collecting food trays, plastic bottles and cans for reuse as raw materials in the manufacturing of new products. Japan has adopted a technology to efficiently recover electricity and fuel from biomass waste. It attempts to recycle their waste into feed, fertilizer and gas fuel by methane fermentation process.

Solid Waste Management in Germany

The objective of the German government's policy on waste is to achieve a recycling based economy that conserves resources and reduces adverse impacts on the environment. The aim is to increase and optimise the efficient use of raw materials, to maximise recovery quotas and to permanently remove from our environment any residual waste that can no longer be used. This will lead to a substance management within closed substance cycles, i.e. turning today's trash into tomorrow's treasure. Activities on waste are part of the Federal Ministry for the

Environment, Nature Conservation and Nuclear Safety's action programme to increase the productivity of resources.

Waste management legislation is based on European law, German federal law, the regional laws of the federal states and the statutes of the local authority. It is also based on the precautionary principle, the polluter-pay principle and the principle of co-operation. The main pillar is the Closed Substance Cycle and Waste Management Act. Through this act, industry and the commercial sector have been made responsible for the recovery of waste, i.e. they also have to bear the costs. All waste from private households and waste for disposal from other generators has to be passed on to waste institutions subject to public law. For waste destined for disposal, it has been stipulated that priority should be given to disposal within Germany (self-sufficiency principle), whilst waste destined for recovery underlies the free movement of goods within the European Union.

Today, the waste industry in Germany employs over 200,000 people and generates an annual turnover in excess of •40 billion. Various activities on capacity-building, education, training and awareness are carried out on federal level, State level and community level and also by the private sector and non-governmental organisations. Trade unions and private-sector businesses play an active role in shaping the integration of ecological and business concerns in waste management.

Solid Waste Management in Singapore

The small island nation of Singapore - where waste production rose six-fold from 1970 to 2000, has been facing the challenge of handling waste with limited space. Integrated planning and the goals towards zero waste and zero landfill are now turning the tide on waste.

Singapore is a highly urbanized and industrialized small island nation with a land area of 697 km^2 and a population of 4.2 million. It has four waste-to-energy refuse incineration plants and an offshore sanitary landfill for the disposal of non-combustible waste.

To address the potential waste problem, Singapore has set up an integrated solid waste management system in the past three decades that incorporates recycling, collection and disposal. Working hand in hand with key stakeholders in the private and government sectors as well as the general public, Singapore's National Environment Agency (NEA) has formulated a range of strategies and programmes to achieve its objectives for curbing waste growth and supporting sustainable waste management.

Starting at the top of the 'waste hierarchy', naturally a key objective is to reduce waste production. The country has also adopted specific measures to minimize waste generation, such as the careful selection of design and construction methods that minimize waste production. For example, contractors who want to tender for large government projects are required to be ISO-14001 certified.

By undertaking these measures, Singapore is taking a big leap forward to achieve the ultimate goal of 'Towards Zero Landfill'. And it is not resting on its achievements so far. The next step is to raise the bar by striving for zero waste. This means moving upstream to avoid waste at source and bringing the producers of waste on board to collaborate with the NEA and the community to reduce waste.

Solid Waste Management in Malaysia

Malaysia surges ahead with a renewed focus on urbanization and industrialization to maintain sustainable growth and development. However, with the ever-increasing population, rapid urbanization and industrialization, the waste generation as a result of natural resource consumption is also rising at the equal pace. The country's build-up of waste result in tremendous land and air pollution, health problems for communities and bottlenecks to economic growth. Taken together, the problem of poor waste management in Malaysia is one of the nation's biggest issues to date.

For years, local and national governments have been trying to curb the flow of garbage on sidewalks, into landfills, over hillsides and through rivers, but Malaysia's turbulent pace of change has made that process extremely difficult.

Disposal of millions of tonnes of untreated garbage by the municipal bodies in the country leads to health issues and environmental degradation. Waste management has become a major challenge for the federal government, State governments and its municipal bodies. In 2016, Malaysia produced an average of 38,000 tonnes of solid waste daily, which include 15,000 tonnes of food waste. Therefore, the Malaysian government has committed to improve the quality solid waste management over the last decade.

Due to increasing lack of space for new landfills, authorities in major cities in Malaysia are attempting to find out other waste management approaches. Among them is an approach to move away from unsanitary landfills due to greenhouse gas (GHG) emissions such as methane and carbon dioxide.

Incineration is the second mostly used method to manage waste in Malaysia. It is one of the most effective means of dealing with various types of wastes. Despite being an attractive technological option for waste management, this type of combustion-based process for municipal solid waste treatment is a subject of intense debate around the world (Achillas et al., 2011). In the absence of effective controls, harmful pollutants such as dioxins may emit into the air, land and water which may affect human health and natural environment. Although incineration of municipal waste coupled with material and energy recovery can form an essential part of an integrated waste management system, yet strict controls are required to prevent its negative impacts on human health and natural environment (Misra and Pandey, 2005).

From the above description about the solid waste management practices at various countries both developed and developing, it was found that solid waste management was their challenging task due to the unprecedented growth of population, urbanisation and industrialisation. More research and development activities should be done in finding the innovative way of managing the solid waste. At this outset the innovative and best practices followed in the management of solid waste is presented below, which can be followed by other countries.

3.3 Innovative and Best Practices in Solid Waste Management

Deposit Refund Scheme

In EU and UK, a scheme called "Deposit Refund Scheme" was celebrated as the commendable scheme for solid waste management worldwide. Under the scheme, consumers who are returning their used bottles or cans will be given incentives. It is done with a view to reduce pressure on landfills and to increase the life cycle of the goods. If the scheme is extended to cover all types of goods that will definitely increase the scope of reuse and recycling. The success of the scheme enables its replication across different countries in the customized way.

Zero Waste Technology

In a region viz. Kamikatsu, in Japan 80 percent of the wastes are recycled and only 20 percent will be disposed in landfills. The residents were sensitised to segregate and bring their waste to recycling centres by themselves. No garbage trucks were found in the particular region. It can be a role model to the entire world in waste management, since they proclaimed themselves as "Zero Waste Region" by 2020.

Waste to Energy Technology

Sweden has been celebrated as a landmark in the solid waste management, which attained 99 percent recycling and barely one percent will go for landfills. Since their landfill sites remain vacant, the country adopted to import waste from other countries. Major portion of the household waste was converted into energy by using the 'Waste to Energy Technology'. By using the WTE, electricity, biogas and bio-fertilizers were obtained. The households and firms were used to segregate their wastes into hazardous waste and recyclable materials.

Clean Homes Clean City

The Coastal town of Alappuzha in Kerala has been included in the Report of United Nations of five global cities, which have successfully managed their solid waste. 100 percent segregation was achieved in all the wards of the city by implementing the project called *Nirmala Bhavanam Nirmala Nagaram* (Clean Homes Clean City) since November 2012. The waste management has been decentralized in the city by adopting decentralised composting system. Around 80 percent of the households in the city had their own biogas plants.

Specific Innovations

The developed countries like USA, Germany, Australia, Brazil and Columbia have adopted specific innovations towards sustainable waste management. The USA has adopted an eco – friendly robotic technology to the clean the Baltimore River. Australia has made innovation in collecting the waste by using 'Smart Belly Bins' which segregate waste at the source itself and then compost and treat the waste. Columbia is offering incentives and rewards to public in the form of movie tickets and vouchers, who were depositing their used plastic bottles and its caps by using vending machines called ECOBOT.

The innovations and best practices adopted at various parts of world in the waste management should be publicized through various forms of media in order to motivate the other countries to improve their waste management status.

3.4 Status of Municipal Solid Waste Management in India

Solid waste generated in urban areas of India have been collected from the Ministry of New and Renewal Energy and furnished in this section. The details of State wise solid waste generation have been presented. The total solid waste generated per day (in tonnes) and the total solid waste generated (in metric tonnes) per annum have been collected and given in this section. The data relating to solid waste generation have been obtained as on November 2017. Accordingly, these data have been furnished in the following table:

Table 3.2: State-Wise Solid Waste Generation

(As on November 2017)

S.No.	*State*	*Total Waste Generation (MT/D)*	*Total Waste Generation (in MT/ Perannum)*
1	Andhra Pradesh	6,525	23.82
2	Andaman & Nicobar Islands	115	0.42
3	Arunachal Pradesh	181	0.66
4	Assam	1,134	4.14
5	Bihar	1,192	4.35
6	Chandigarh UT	340	1.24
7	Chhattisgarh	1,959	7.15
8	Daman & Diu	23	0.08
9	Dadra & Nagar Haveli	58	0.21
10	NCT of Delhi	10,500	38.33
11	Goa	240	0.88
12	Gujarat	10,145	37.03

13	Haryana	4,514	16.48
14	Himachal Pradesh	342	1.25
15	Jammu & Kashmir	1,792	6.54
16	Jharkhand	2,451	8.95
17	Karnataka	10,000	36.5
18	Kerala	1,576	5.75
19	Madhya Pradesh	6,424	23.45
20	Maharashtra	22,570	82.38
21	Manipur	176	0.64
22	Meghalaya	268	0.98
23	Mizoram	201	0.73
24	Nagaland	342	1.25
25	Odisha	2,460	8.98
26	Puducherry UT	495	1.81
27	Punjab	4,100	14.97
28	Rajasthan	6,500	23.73
29	Sikkim	89	0.32
30	Tamil Nadu	15,547	56.75
31	Telangana	7,371	26.9
32	Tripura	421	1.54
33	Uttar Pradesh	15,500	56.58
34	Uttarakhand	1,400	5.11
35	West Bengal	8,675	31.66
	Total	**145626**	**531.56**

Source: Ministry of New and Renewable Energy.

Maharashtra State ranks first in terms of total waste generation followed by Tamil Nadu in India. Maharashtra's percentage share is about 15.5 percent in the total waste generated in India. About 10.7 was the percentage share of Tamil Nadu. The urbanisation and increase in population has been spotted as one of the major reasons attributing this fact. The Central Pollution Board has suggested that States generating wastes more than 500 MT per day have to formulate their customized action plan, which provides advice to local bodies for setting up scientific waste processing and disposal facilities.

3.5 Practices of Solid Waste Management at Major Cities in India

Solid Waste Management in Delhi

For the National Capital Territory of Delhi (NCT), a separate legislation viz. Solid Waste Management Bye-Laws 2018 has been issued in the year 2018 on January 15th. It comes under Section 5 of the Environmental Protection Act. It is applicable to all the five municipal corporations in Delhi comprising 280 wards.

As per the bye law it is the duty of the waste generator to sort and segregate the waste before disposal as biodegradables, non biodegradables and domestic hazardous waste under Section 5. The authorized waste pickers were allowed to collect the bulk wastes from hotels and commercial centres. The Section 6 of the byelaw consist rules regarding door to door collection of segregated wastes and its transportation. The Section 7 of the byelaw deals with secondary storage of waste and transporting them into recycling centres for further processing.

The total solid waste generated is about 14,000 tons per day in Delhi. In Delhi the per capita waste generation is about 600 grams per day. Of the total waste collected, nearly 6000 tons per day have been processed and managed scientifically by three incinerators and two composting units. The remaining quantum of waste which is around 4500 tons per day had been simply dumped in dumping yards viz. Okhla, Bhalswa and Ghazipur.

Solid Waste Management in Mumbai

Mumbai Metropolitan Region (MMR) spread over 4355 sq. Km comprising seven Municipal Corporations.

Mumbai has been divided into 3 divisions for its administrative purpose as Division I, II, and III. The population of the city is very huge which is increasing on a daily basis, generates huge amount of waste. Mumbai generated around 7025 MT of waste per day. The waste management of the city is formally entrusted with the Mumbai Corporation of Greater Mumbai (MCGM). At present the garbage collected from households was attempted to be disposed off in four main dumping sites in the city, Viz. Gorai, Deonar, Mulund and kanjumarg.

A programme viz., Parisar Vikas programme was implemented by the Mumbai based NGO, in which female rag pickers were organised into cooperatives and trainned in the areas of waste collection, handling, processing and transportation. A community based model viz. advanced locality management was implemented in Mumbai to enable for decentralised waste management. It is the principle of partnership and co-operation on a local level involving various stakeholders viz. NGOs, local residents and municipal authorities. There are 658 ALMS in all wards of Mumbai.

The current municipal solid waste management system in Mumbai is found to be inadequate and unscientific due to challenges like lack of coordination and lack of systematic approach at all levels.

Solid Waste Management in Kolkata

In most parts of the world today, solid wastes are disposed of either in open dumps or sanitary landfills, or by incineration. As incineration and sanitary land filling are expensive, both in initial investment and throughout their operation, their use is mostly confined to developed countries, while open dumping is the method used in economically developing countries, mainly due to its simplicity and low cost. India's traditional means of disposing of solid waste has been to dump it at these open sites, or at sea. Solid waste management has become a considerable issue, in addition to other environmental problems, especially for densely populated cities in developing countries.

Kolkata province consists of three municipalities: Kolkata Municipal Corporation, Bidhan Nagar Municipal

Corporation and Dum Municipal Corporation. All operations of solid waste management (SWM) in these areas are performed under four heads – sweeping, collection, transportation and disposal.

In the city area, street cleaning and collection involves collection of MSW from the streets (road sweeping) and households in handcarts. Thereafter, the waste is dumped at one of the 664 collection points (primary collection). MSW is then loaded into transportation vehicles (trucks) (secondary collection), which transport the waste (transfer) to disposal sites.

In Kolkata province and its towns, open dumping is the only option that is presently used for the management of the MSW. Kolkata's municipal solid waste generally consists of waste generated from residential, commercial and institutional areas and is not sorted at the source, but stored in the same waste containers. The dimensions and numbers of containers vary according to the width of the street and the quantity of the waste generated. The total number of waste bins in Kolkata is 664. Solid wastes stored in waste bins are collected and transported to the open dump area by vehicles belonging to the municipality of Kolkata.

Solid Waste Management in Jaipur

Solid Waste Management is a major concern worldwide. Inadequate handling of generated solid waste causes serious hazards to environment as well as living beings. This worldwide problem is also predominating in Jaipur city also. There is no proper mechanism in Jaipur city for the treatment of solid waste generated, which leads to dumping of waste in open areas which causes various problems to environment as well as humans living in that vicinity.

It was seen that there was lack of community garbage collection facility in slums. Slum dwellers dump their garbage nearby the living area. The refuse bins in old Jaipur area were very dirty and overflowing. People often threw the garbage outside the garbage bins. The inconvenience of huge garbage on streets and sorting by the sweepers or moving stray animals on the streets represent very ugly scene.

It was observed at many places in the morning, thick black smoke spread over large areas on the roads due to burning of fallen leaves, plastics and other wastes. Most of the drains along the road and even main sewer lines near Mother Dairy, Bais Godam, Durgapura and Pratapnagar were found blocked due to indiscriminate dumping of garbage.

Solid Waste Management in Bengaluru

The Municipal Solid Waste (MSW) consists of organic and inorganic waste materials generated by various societal activities. The improper disposal of MSW pollutes all the vital components of the living environment, i.e., air, land, and water. Bengaluru is located in the southeast of Indian State. It is situated at 12.97°N 77.56°E and covers an area of 2,190 square kilometers at an average elevation of 920 meters.

Bengaluru city experiences a moderate weather throughout the year. In summer from March to May the maximum temperature rise up to 38°C. In winter months the temperature varies between 28°C and 32°C. The annual rainfall is about 900 mm.

Currently, Bengaluru city generates around 5000 MT/day of MSW at an average of 0.5 kg/day/per capita with a population of about 10.18 million. Bengaluru city is facing serious problems due to existing disposal practices of generated waste incurring high cost due to lack of proper infrastructural facilities, also the open dumping in the expanding zone of the city poses serious problems to the groundwater quality due to improper leachate management. However, with an increasing population and the growing necessities of the Information Technology (IT) sector, the local authorities are struggling to provide the proper solid waste management system to a satisfactory level. Recently, the authorities have taken initiatives and measures to organize municipal solid waste management (MSWM) sector. Bengaluru city being a historical city has several narrow streets and gulleys, high population density and has pockets of rural area which have been amalgamated with developed areas, posing serious problems for collection and transport of Municipal waste. The phenomenal growths of vehicles on roads make the task even more difficult.

Presently, the Bruhat Bengaluru Mahanagara Palike (BBMP), the agency vested with responsibility of collection and disposal of solid waste, is engaged in a series of approaches such as involvement of citizen, investment in infrastructure and technology, as well as monitoring the various systems that are involved in managing the present mix of actions and techniques.

In Bengaluru, at present only 10% of the waste is recycled. The 0.5 kg/capita/day is proposed as waste generation rate for Bengaluru city. From past two decades of economic growth (since 1990), the composition of India's urban wastes has changed. In Bengaluru, presently the waste generation is about 5000 metric tons and the waste generation is likely to grow over the coming years. Going by the present trend of increase in the quantity of waste, the waste quantity projected to increase in the next 20 years.

Source segregation is still a concern in Bengaluru though awareness in picking up is slow. BBMP manages about 30% of MSW and 70% of MSW activity starting from primary collection to disposal has been outsourced.

The BBMP has assigned the primary and secondary collection of waste and transportation activity to Self Help Groups (SHG's) which are basically below poverty. The landfill sites are operated by the private sector based on public-private partnership (PPP).

Presently, Bengaluru does not have any scientific treatment facilities for the management of solid waste generated by municipalities and industries around Bengaluru. This has led to the development of several illegal and unauthorized dump sites in Bengaluru.

Table 3.3: Solid Waste Generated in the State of Tamil Nadu

(District wise)

S. No.	Districts	Corporation		Municipalities		Town Panchayats		Total	
		No.	Solid Waste generated TPD	No.	Solid Waste generated TPD	No.	Solid Waste generated TPD	No.	Solid Waste generated TPD
1	Chennai	1	6404	-	-	-	-	1	6404
2	Coimbatore	1	890	3	107	37	210	41	1207
3	Cuddalore	-	-	5	228	16	15	21	275
4	Dindigul	1	110	3	74	23	68	27	252
5	Erode	1	275	4	76	42	159	47	510
6	Dharmapuri & Krishnagiri	-	-	3	158	17	40	20	198
7	Karur	-	-	2	139	11	31	13	170
8	Madurai	1	680	3	55	9	33	13	764
9	Kanchipuram	-	-	9	442	15	363	24	805
10	Nagapatinam	-	-	4	97	8	22	11	119
11	Namakkal	-	-	5	146	19	65	24	211
12	Thiruvarur	-	-	4	52	7	6.8	11	74
13	Kanyakumari	-	-	4	134	56	59	60	193
14	Ooty	-	-	4	68	11	15	15	75
15	Pudukkottai	-	-	2	55	8	23	10	78
16	Salem	1	400	4	73	33	120	38	543
17	Ramnad	-	-	4	100	7	35	11	135
18	Sivagangai	-	-	3	69	12	36	15	105
19	Thanjavur	1	120	2	55	22	75	25	250
20	Theni	-	-	6	77	22	72	28	226
21	Thoothukudi	1	205	2	44	19	30	22	279
22	Tirunelveli	1	180	7	121	36	38	44	339
23	Tiruppur	1	508	5	117	16	53	22	678
24	Tiruvallur	-	-	5	241	10	26	15	267
25	Tiruvannamalai	-	-	4	131	10	32	14	330
26	Tiruchirappalli	1	436	3	45	16	71	20	552
27	Ariyalur	-	-	3	49	6	11	4	60
28	Perambalur	-	-	1	24	4	10	5	34
29	Vellore	1	230	11	291	16	41	28	562
30	Virudhunagar	-	-	7	234	9	27	16	261
31	Villupuram	-	-	3	123	15	68	18	159
	Total	12	10438	124	3703	528	1901	664	14588

Source: Tamil Nadu Pollution Control Board, Nov 2017

3.6 Municipal Solid Waste Management in Tamil Nadu

In Tamil Nadu, there are 12 Municipal Corporations, 124 Municipalities and 528 Town Panchayats. The details of solid waste generated – Corporation wise, Municipality wise and Town Panchayat wise have been presented in this section. The solid wastes generated have been furnished in tonnes per day.

Chennai Corporation ranks first in terms of solid waste generation when compared to other districts, which shares about 34 percent in the total waste generated in the State. In India Chennai Corporation ranks first in terms of per capita waste generation at 0.71 kg followed by Kolkatta (0.66 Kg.). Due to the higher population density, commercial and industrial activities Chennai Corporation discharged a huge amount of solid wastes. It generates about 6404 tonnes of waste per day of which 25 percent is recyclable, 60 percent organic waste and 10 percent hazardous waste. In terms of waste generation, Coimbatore Corporation occupies the second place with a percentage share 8.52. Salem Corporation occupies the sixth position in terms of solid waste generation.

There are 12 Municipal Corporations in the State of Tamil Nadu including Chennai, Coimbatore, Dindigul, Erode, Madurai, Salem, Thanjavur, Thoothukudi, Tirunelveli, Tiruppur, Trichy and Vellore. The details of population and the amount of solid waste generation, collection, disposal and treatment per day have been furnished in this section.

Table 3.4: Generation of Municipal Solid Waste in the Corporations of Tamil Nadu

S. No.	*Name of Corporation*	*Population in Lakhs*	*Solid Waste Generated TPD*	*Solid Waste Collected TPD*	*Solid Waste Treated*	*Solid Waste Disposed TPD*
1	Chennai	62.5	6404	6404	—	6404
2	Coimbatore	12.621	890	890	590	180
3	Dindigul	2.07	110	110	10	100

4	Erode	4.98	275	275	120	155
5	Madurai	14.62	680	640	350	180
6	Salem	8.31	400	400320	290320	1302
7	Thanjavur	7.43	120	114	—	114
8	Thoothukudi	4.1	205	205	—	205
9	Tirunelveli	4.99	180	170	—	150
10	Tiruppur	8.77	508	508	—	508
11	Trichy	7.966	436	416	100	316
12	Vellore	4.234	230	210	—	207

Source: Tamil Nadu Pollution Control Board, Nov 2017.

The above table clearly indicates the prevalence of gap between the amounts of waste generated, disposed and treated in the corporations. It shows the inefficiency of solid waste management activities undertaken by the corporations in the State.

Solid Waste Management in Chennai

Chennai the first largest corporation of the State generates about 5400 tonnes of wastes every day. Its per capita waste generation is about 550 gms per day. It is attempted to manage the 80 percent garbage of Chennai Corporation by private conservancy firms. There are 15 zones in Chennai Corporation of which 3 zones have been privatized for municipal solid waste management, 8 zones were in the process to be privatized and the remaining 4 zones were in the hands of corporation. The solid wastes are collected and segregated as recyclable and non-recyclable. Regarding the method of waste collection, for collecting commercial wastes, night conservancy is adopted and for domestic garbage collection, door-to-door collection is done. The recyclable solid wastes in Chennai Municipal Corporation are collected at the household level by the sanitary workers. The primary collection of solid wastes has been made in two phases. In the first phase, the solid wastes are collected by the deputed conservancy workers from 6.30 to 10.30 am in the morning and from 2.30 to 5.00 pm in the evening. The second phase of waste collection is carried out by compactors and tricyles between 6.30 am and 1.30 pm. These wastes are dumped in two dumping yards – Kodungaiyur (269 acres) and Perungudi (260 acres). As an innovative strategy, Chennai Corporation has installed five "Waste to Energy Conversion Plants" with a capacity to feed about 8.80 MT of bio-degradable wastes, of which 54 KWH of electricity is produced per day being used for street lights.

Solid Waste Management in Coimbatore

Coimbatore, the second largest city in Tamil Nadu generates about 815 MT per day. Its per capita waste generation is about 550 gms. The Corporation had four zones with 72 wards. It had its waste disposal site with 654.54 acres. The municipal solid waste management of the corporation has been undertaken with the help of around 7300 sanitary workers. GIS has been used as a tool in the solid waste management system to monitor its waste management activities at the disposal sites. As a new initiative all the urban local bodies were instructed to collect the segregated bio degradable wastes from commercial establishments to convert into bio gas. Under the Clean Cities Championship Campaign an initiative called "Expression of Interest" (EOI) was instigated by the Coimbatore Corporation to improve and strengthen its waste management practices.

Solid Waste Management in Dindigul

Dindigul Corporation generates about 104 MT of solid waste per day with the per capita waste generation of 480 grams per day. In the case of Dindigul, the solid wastes have been collected manually and dumped at disposal yard. The solid wastes are not segregated at source in Dindigul. They are transported to the dumping yard through truck, tippers, dumper-placers and tri-cycles and stored in the dumping yard. The solid wastes dumped are partially composted. As an innovative strategy, an attempt has been made to convert the Corporation's total garbage into manure with a composting plant under the windrow technology, which will be sold by the agriculture department.

Solid Waste Management in Erode

The solid wastes are collected on door-to-door basis in Erode. The method of collection of solid waste here is manual. Erode Municipal Corporation has provided 518 dumper bins across the wards for the storage of solid wastes. There are three dumping yards with an area of 28.87 acres in total viz. Vendipalayam, Vairapalayam and Kasipalayam. On an average 250 MTs of solid wastes are collected throughout the geographical limits of Erode. Out of the total solid waste generated, 120 MTs have been processed by composting at Vendipalayam composting yard and the remaining 130 MTs have been disposed by open dumping. Tractors, trailers, power tillers and push carts have been used for transportation of solid wastes.

Solid Waste Management in Madurai

The Madurai Corporation has four zones with 100 wards. It generates about 548 MT per day with a per capita generation of 406 grams per day. Like other corporations, Madurai Corporation is also not practising any scientific method of disposal. At present all the wastes collected are dumped at a site viz. Vellakkal with 82 acres. The solid waste management followed by Madurai Corporation is the door-to-door collection method of solid wastes using collection bins. The segregation of solid waste is not made at the source level. Madurai Corporation has placed dumper bins in all types of areas – residential, commercial and market areas. These solid wastes are transported by using dumper placers, mobile compactors, tipper lorries and tipper tractors. They have adopted window aerobic method for bio-composting of solid wastes.

They dump the demolition and construction waste on notified low-laying area.

3.7 Municipal Solid Waste Management in Salem Corporation

Salem is a city and a Municipal Corporation in Salem district in the Tamil Nadu State of India. Salem is the fifth largest city in Tamil Nadu in terms of population after Chennai, Coimbatore, Madurai, and Tiruchirappalli respectively. It is the fifth Municipal Corporation and Urban agglomeration commissioned in Tamil Nadu after Chennai (1919), Coimbatore (1981), Madurai (1971) and Tiruchirappalli (1994) respectively. Salem UA has a population of 913188 for the year 2017.

The Centurion Municipality was declared as **Salem City Municipal Corporation** from 1.6.1994. The Salem City Municipal Council celebrated its Centenary in 1966. Fittingly the Municipality was upgraded into a special grade Municipality with effect from 1.4.79. Salem City Municipal limits were further extended by the inclusion of Suramangalam Municipality, Jarikondalampatty Town Panchayat, Kannankurichi Town Panchayat and 21 other Villages. Salem Corporation consists of 60 wards categorized under four Zonal Offices, namely Suramangalam Zone, Hasthampatty Zone, Ammapet Zone and Kondalampatty Zone. The waste management in the city is entrusted with the sanitary inspectors and a team of sanitary supervisors and sanity workers. The aim of the City Municipal Corporation is 100% collection of garbage generated in the city daily. There are 60 sanitary divisions functioning in Salem Corporation. A team of 28 sanitary inspectors, 60 sanitary supervisors and 1922 sanitary workers are engaged in solid waste management activities.

Municipal Solid Waste generation in Salem Corporation has been around 400 tonnes daily. Per capita waste generation is 450 grams per day in the Corporation. Salem Corporation has 60 sanitary divisions covering 91:34 sq.kms and collection of garbage is carried out using door-to-door collection and street bin systems. The solid wastes generated from houses, commercial establishments, roads, streets, drainages markets, hospitals and other establishments were collected, transported and disposed in three stages viz. primary, secondary and tertiary. A practice of source segregation has been adopted in all the wards of Salem Corporation.

Primary Stage

In this process the solid wastes are classified into bio-degradable and non bio- degradable wastes at source, which have been collected daily in the door steps through pushcarts and tricycles. At this stage the wastes were simply used to be stored in dumper bins on temporary basis.

Secondary Stage

In this stage there would be the transportation of collected wastes to compost yards with the help of tractors, dumper bin placers and automatic refuse collectors for further processing.

Tertiary stage

In this final stage, wastes have been attempted to be dumped at compost yard. At present no scientific method of composting has been practiced at Salem Corporation. Wastes have been simply dumped at large piths at the dumping yard located in Chettichavadi village.

Administrative setup of Municipal Solid Waste Management:

The administrative setup of Municipal Solid Waste Management in every municipality is shown in figure 3.1.

Figure 3.1: The Hierarchy of the Staff Municipal Secretary

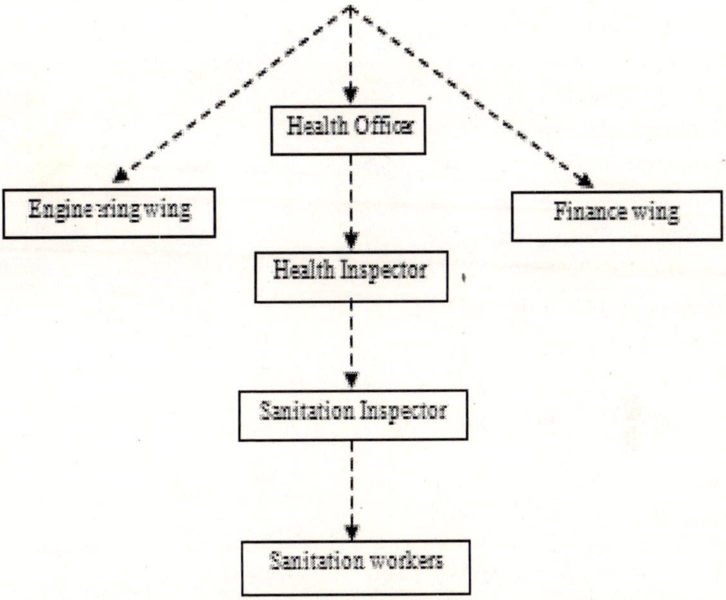

The task of municipal solid waste management is entrusted with two major departments viz. engineering and finance departments headed by the Municipal Secretary. He is at the top position of the municipal solid waste management system. The health officer comes at the next position, who is a medical doctor. He will be assisted by health inspectors and junior health inspectors. The sanitary workers handling wastes work under the sanitation inspectors.

The following tables reveal the details about solid waste management in Salem Corporation.

Table 3.5: Vital Statistics of Salem Corporation Concerning Solid Waste Management

Description	*Numbers*
Area	91.34 sq. Km
No of Wards	60
Population	913188

No. of Households	234264
Commercial Establishments	25504
No. of Slums	200
Slum Households	215314 (2019)
Slum Population	131127
Common Places	85
Educational Institutions – Schools	285
Educational Institutions – Colleges	13
Hotels and Restaurants	62
Lodges	41
Marriage and Community Halls	60
Vegetable Markets	11
Fish Market	1
Slaughter Houses	3
No. of Industries	584
Hospitals	139
Total Road Length	855 km

Source: Salem Corporation, 2017.

The corporation limits consists many of commercial and industrial establishments which accounts for larger generation of solid wastes comprising organic and inorganic wastes.

Table 3.6: Zone wise Population and Number of Households in Salem Corporation

Zones	*2015*		*2017*	
	Population	*Number of Households*	*Population*	*Number of Households*
Suramangalam	239433	66411	246663	67538
Hasthampatty	204097	44682	196614	53553
Ammapet	215271	49127	234287	63275
Kondalampatty	225945	55094	235624	49898
Total	884746	215314	913188	234264

Source: Salem Corporation, 2017

Of the four zones, in terms of both population and number of households, Suramanagalam Zone ranked first next to Ammapet Zone.

Table 3.7: Waste Generation by Corporation

	Suramangalam	*Hasthampatty*	*Ammapet*	*Kondalampatty*
No. of Wards	14	14	16	16
Waste Generation	103.85	95.22	99.98	101.16
Percapita Waste Generation 400 gms Per day				

Source: Salem Corporation, 2018.

Of the four zones, Suramangalam zone consisting 14 wards generates huge quantity of wastes which shares about 26 percent of the total waste generated in the corporation followed by Kondalampatty zone (25 percent). In terms of population and number of households also Suramangalam zone occupies the major share. The concentration of commercial and industrial centres viz. central bus stand, railway station, Uzhavar Sandahi, fish market, TANMAG, SAGOSERVE and SIPCOT in Suramanglam also accounts for the larger waste generation in the zone. The least waste generator is Hasthampatty Zone which shares about 24 percent of the total waste is due to its least population concentration when compared to other Zones.

Table 3.8: Ward wise Population, Households and Waste Generation in Salem Corporation

Ward	*Households*	*Population*	*Waste generation*
1	4927	21791	5.30
2	5773	26054	7.08
3	6612	29681	8.50
4	3902	15118	7.85
5	6903	28038	8.68
6	4626	19392	5.99
7	3947	16813	9.40
8	6680	29711	9.57
9	6945	31865	8.95
10	3395	13463	6.71

11	2786	8730	4.69
12	3712	13144	7.29
13	2914	11261	8.71
14	3395	13198	5.50
15	3265	9852	6.51
16	3654	12795	6.19
17	2787	9804	7.60
18	4109	15741	8.93
19	3515	10810	5.25
20	2253	8997	4.07
21	3475	15037	1.04
22	3450	15049	6.95
23	4209	18804	8.46
24	5049	20456	9.99
25	3920	15696	8.67
26	2981	11706	7.92
27	3692	13174	5.55
28	3190	12549	9.99
29	3246	11118	6.15
30	3652	11871	8.48
31	2350	5617	3.45
32	2357	9290	10.86
33	2646	9093	11.0
34	3044	10542	5.15
35	5012	19281	7.12
36	3854	11774	5.47
37	5384	26447	8.32
38	2675	10521	4.52
39	3002	10729	3.63
40	4539	17664	4.71
41	3114	11364	5.82
42	2865	7279	4.73
43	3526	16602	3.91
44	4256	19644	4.39
45	3082	11543	7.71
46	3246	10719	5.93
47	3523	13862	6.54
48	2627	9044	4.37
49	2631	10731	4.49
50	9015	38563	13.0
51	2754	8130	4.36
52	2582	8524	3.50

53	4502	16280	7.41
54	3652	12054	5.03
55	3895	15122	6.89
56	3002	9988	4.64
57	4115	15662	7.16
58	4682	17175	6.50
59	4456	17666	5.36
60	4912	20561	8.27
Total	**234264**	**913188**	**400 MT / day**

Source: Salem Corporation, 2018.

There exists wide variation in population, number of households and amount of waste generation among 60 wards in Salem Corporation. The total waste generation by the corporation is 400 MT per day. The two wards viz. VOC market and Maniyanur in Ammapet zone and Kondalampatty zone respectively generates the largest quantity of wastes. The concentration of commercial centres along with higher population accounts for larger generation of wastes in those wards. The other major wards which generate huge quantum of waste includes Milk Market, New Bus Stand, Old Bus Stand, Bazaar, Gugai and Shevapat.

Table 3.9: Correlation Coefficients

		Population	Waste Generation
Population	Pearson correlation	1	0.562**
	Sig.(2-tailed)		.000
	N	60	60
Waste generation	Pearson correlation	0.562**	1
	Sig.(2-tailed)	.000	
	N	60	60

** Correlation is significant at the 0.01 level (2-tailed).

To find out the relationship between population and waste generation in all the 60 wards of Salem Corporation, correlation has been applied. It was found that there was a significant relationship between the population and waste generation in the wards of Salem Corporation since the p value is less than 0.001. A moderate of amount of correlation was found between the two variables viz. population and waste generation (0.562).

Table 3.10: Composition of Solid Waste in Salem Corporation

Waste composition		*Quantity in Metric tonnes*
Total Solid Waste		400
i)	Domestic Garbage Waste	280
ii)	Industrial Waste	Nil
iii)	Market Waste	20
iv)	Street Sweeping Waste	40
v)	Commercial Waste	60
vi)	Construction Material Waste	5

Source: Salem Corporation, 2018.

Figure 3.2: Composition of Solid Waste in Salem Corporation

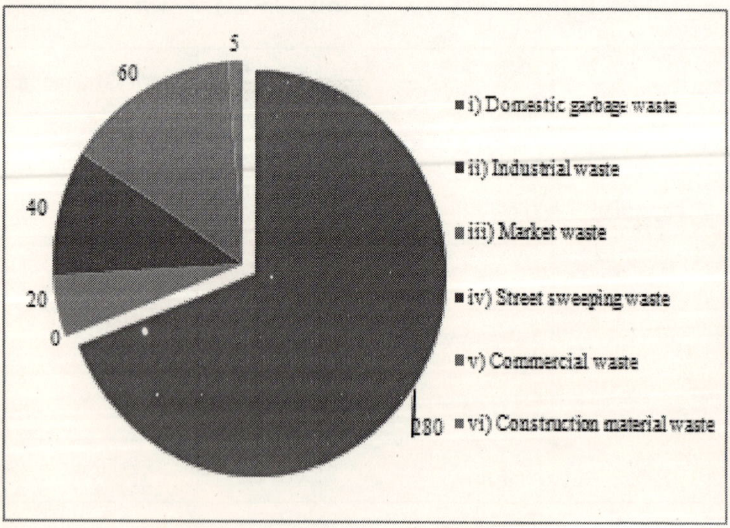

Regarding the composition of municipal solid waste in Salem Corporation, the domestic garbage waste share huge i.e. 70 percent of the total waste. The commercial waste accounts 15 percent share. The nil share of industrial waste doesn't mean that industrial waste of the corporation is zero, but it was due to the non – separation of industrial waste by the municipal authorities. The scope of recycling is large in Salem Corporation, since the domestic garbage occupies a major share of the total waste generated.

Table 3.11: Characteristics of Municipal Solid Waste in Salem Corporation

Nature of Waste	*Quantity (in Metric tons per day)*
Bio Degradable Waste	241
Bio Methanation Potential Waste	18
Non – Bio degradable Waste	17
Silt / Inert	124
Total	**400**

Source: Salem Corporation, 2018.

Figure 3.3: Characteristics of Municipal Solid Waste in Salem Corporation

(in metric tons per day)

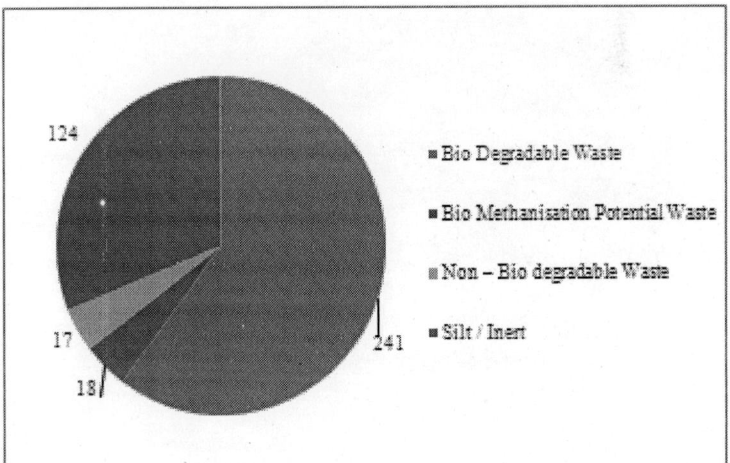

The above table 3.11 describes the composition of solid waste on its chemical properties in Salem Corporation. Of the total waste 60 percent of the waste is biodegradable in the Corporation followed by silt/inert (31 percent).

Table 3.12: Non-Bio Degradable Waste Composition in Salem Corporation

Components	*Weight in Kg*	*% by Weight*
Paper	12000	70.42
Plastics	3360	19.71
Rubber / Rexin	600	3.52
Iron waste	1000	5.86
Glass	80	0.46
Total	**17040**	**100**

Source: Salem Corporation, 2018.

Figure 3.4: Non-Bio Degradable Waste Composition in Salem Corporation

(Percentage by Weight)

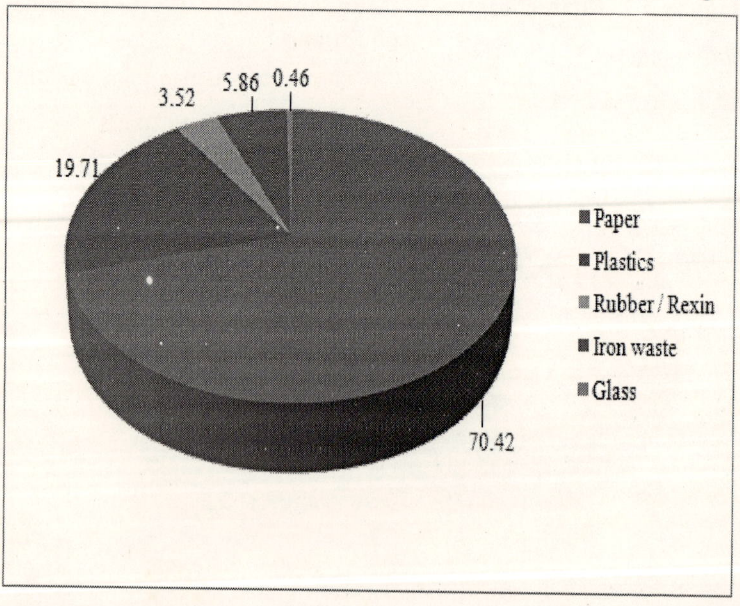

In the category of non-biodegradable waste, paper occupies a major share followed by plastics in Salem Corporation. In the developing country like India 80 percent of the total consumption of plastic and paper is discarded as waste, of which nearly 40 percent remains uncollected. The real problem is the consumption of single use plastics, which are not effectively collected. This may find its own way into landfills, unauthorised garbage dumps or it may remain simply uncollected on road sides.

Table 3.13: Commercial Establishments in Salem Corporation

Commercial Establishments	*Numbers*
Schools	287
Hotels	62
Markets	11
Marriage Halls	52
Parks	17
Hospitals	139
Bus stands	2

Source: Salem Corporation, 2018.

The huge concentration of commercial activities in the Corporation results in the larger amount of commercial waste generated in the Corporation next to domestic wastes. The larger number of schools, hospitals, hotels and marriage halls accounts for greater share in the total amount of commercial waste generated by the Corporation.

Table 3.14: Personnel Involved in Municipal Solid Waste Management in Salem Corporation

Staff Details / Designation		*Numbers*
Class – I		
	City Health Officer	1
Class – II		
	Assistant Executive Engineers	5

Class – III		
i)	Sanitary inspectors	9
ii)	Sanitary supervisors	60
iii)	Drivers	84
Class – IV 1237		
i)	Sanitary Workers employed by the Corporation	
ii)	Contracted Sanitary Workers	685
	Total	**2081**

Source: Salem Corporation, 2018.

The waste management in the city is entrusted with the sanitary inspectors and a team of sanitary supervisors and sanity workers. The aim of the City Municipal Corporation is 100% collection of garbage generated in the city daily. There are 60 Sanitary Divisions functioning in Salem Corporation. A team of nine sanitary inspectors, 60 sanitary supervisors and 1922 sanitary workers are engaged in solid waste management activities. Of the total sanitary workers 64 percent were corporation workers and the remaining are working under private contractors.

Table 3.15: Types of Equipments and Vehicles used for Waste Collection

Equipments and Vehicles	*Numbers*
Compactors	20
Pumper Placers	6
Tipper Lorries	8
Tractors	12
Mini Autos	8
Hook Loaders with – 6 bins	1
Pushcart with Four bins	497
Battery Operated Vehicles	29
Compactor Bins	330

Source: Salem Corporation, 2018.

Regarding vehicles used for solid waste management in Salem Corporation, it may be concluded that the

Corporation had been well equipped with the sophisticated vehicles for the transportation of the waste.

Table 3.16: Details of Waste Collection

Description	ULB		Privatization		Total
	Residential	Commercial	Residential	Commercial	
Waste collected per day in MT	215	20	100	65	400
Total waste in MT	235		165		400
Waste collection in %	58.75		41.25		100 %

Source: Salem Corporation, 2018.

Of the total waste generated by the Corporation nearly 59 percent has been collected by the Corporation and the remaining collection has been privatized.

Table 3.17: Generation of Waste and Collection Efficiency of Salem Corporation

Year	*Actual Collected Waste for Disposal MT/ Day*	*Actual Generated Waste MT / Day*
2010	330	330
2011	345	345
2012	350	350
2013	360	360
2014	365	365
2015	375	375
2016	385	385
2017	390	390
2018	400	400

Source: Salem Corporation, 2018. .

Figure 3.5: Generation of Waste and Collection Efficiency of Salem Corporation

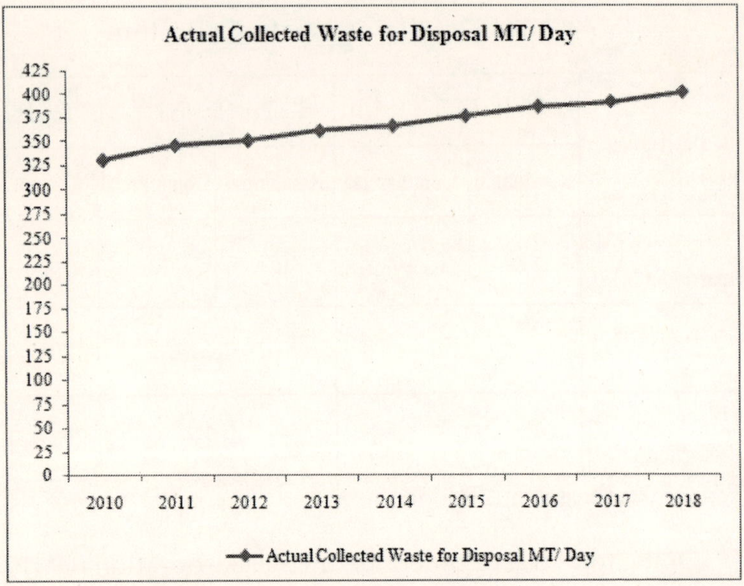

An increasing trend has been observed in the quantum of solid waste generated in the corporation from 2010 to 2018. Surprisingly no gap has been observed between the actual waste generated and collected. It shows 100 percent efficiency in collection of waste by the corporation. Though the Corporation is efficient in the collection of the waste, the menace of solid waste pollution is huge in the city, due to its inefficiency in terms of disposal and management.

Table 3.18: Waste Generation by Salem Corporation from 2010 to 2018

Year	*Residential Waste (MT)*	*Market Waste (MT)*	*Street Sweeping Waste (MT)*	*Commercial Waste (MT)*	*Total (MT)*
2010	231	16.5	33	49.5	330
2011	241.5	17.25	34.5	51.75	345
2012	245	17.5	35	52.5	350
2013	252	18	36	54	360

2014	255.5	18.25	36.5	54.75	365
2015	262.5	18.75	37.5	56.25	375
2016	269.5	19.25	38.5	57.75	385
2017	273	19.5	39	58.5	390
2018	280	20	40	60	400

Source: Salem Corporation, 2018.

Figure 3.6: Waste Generation by Salem Corporation from 2010 to 2018

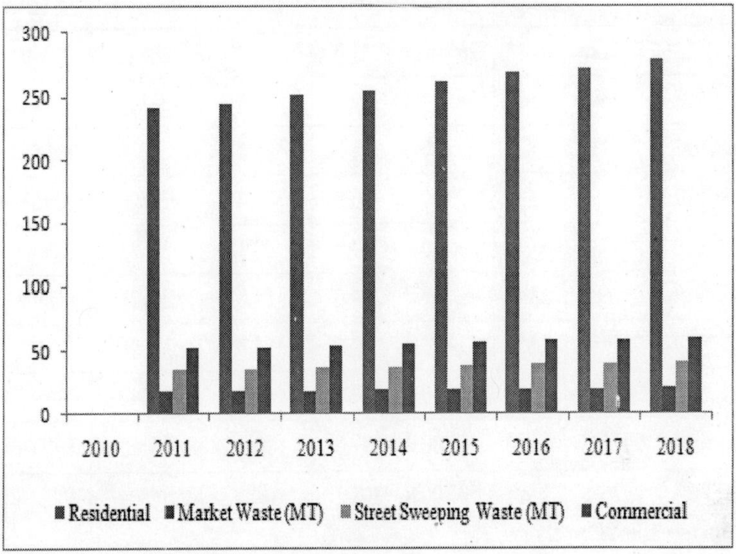

Over the period from 2010 to 2018, the category of residential waste occupied the major share and had also shown a raising trend. The share of commercial waste occupies the second place in its quantity.

Table 3.19: Projection of Population and Generation of Solid Waste in Salem Corporation

Year	Population	Rate of Increase in Generation of Waste	Estimated Quantity in MT/ Day	Estimated Qty of Organic Waste in MT/ Day	Estimated Qty of Inert Waste to be land filled in MT/ day	Estimated Qty of inert waste to be land filled in MT/ year	Cumulative Total Waste in MT / Year
2014	873436	0.415	365.00	222.0	74.0	26640	26640
2015	886687	0.425	375.00	229.2	76.4	27504	54144
2016	899937	0.430	385.00	235.2	78.4	28224	82368
2017	913188	0.435	390.00	240.0	80.0	28800	11168
2018	926438	0.440	400.00	247.8	82.3	29628	140836
2019	939688	0.445	424.00	254.4	84.8	30528	171364
2020	952938	0.450	434.00	260.0	86.8	31248	202612
2021	966188	0.455	445.00	267.0	89.0	32040	234652
2022	979438	0.500	496.00	297.6	99.2	35712	270364
2023	992688	0.505	507.00	304.2	101.4	36504	306868

Source: Salem Corporation, 2018.

The trend in solid waste generation in the corporation has been projected to rise in an alarming rate in the future years. The projected increase in population along with the commercial and industrial activities play a major role in increasing the quantum of solid waste in the corporation. Due to the ban of plastics from the year (January) 2019 by the Tamil Nadu Government, this trend may change. The percentage share of inorganic waste, whose disposal and management was the real menace will be definitely reduced after the enforcement of the rule.

Figure 3.7 : Projection of Population and Generation of Solid Waste in Salem Corporation

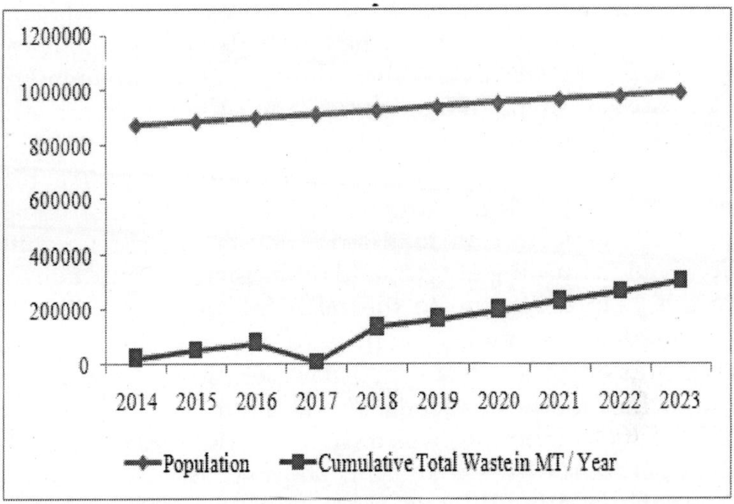

At present in Salem Corporation around 400 MT solid wastes were collected from four zones in Salem Corporation and dumped at Chetticahvadi yard which runs around 100 acres. It is about 16 kms away from Salem city. No scientific method of management has been followed in the dumping yard. A method of open dumping at huge pits has been followed in the site as a method of disposal and management. In the interview with the Corporation officials it was found that only a meagre portion of waste has been attempted to be segregated as bio degradable and non – biodegradable. Prior to the year 2015, the municipal wastes of the corporation were used to be dumped at four yards viz. Erumapalayam, Suramangalam, Veeranam and Maniyanur. In the past 50 years since the dumping began, around 2 lakh MT of solid waste were dumped at Erumapalayam, 26 acre was used as a dumping yard.

In the year 2012, a Modern Scientific Solid Waste Management Plant was started at Chettichavadi yard with the public and private partnership. Of the total waste generated in the corporation only 40 percent of the waste was used to be disposed at Chettichavadi plant. The remaining were attempted to be dumped at Erumapalayam and other dumping yards. The residents at Chetticahvadi village protested against the dumping and management of wastes in their village, due to the problem of air and ground water contamination. Corporation health officials also admitted that environmental pollution was a big problem due to the burning of garbage and had instructed sanitary inspectors to take strict action against persons involved in burning of tyres and other chemical substances. In the year 2014, due to the outbreak of sudden fire at the solid waste management yard at Chettichavadi, the Corporation officials stopped its operation. Later it was found that many misdeeds by the plant from the time it started its functioning was a cause for the incident. Since the operation of the plant was stopped, the Corporation faced many difficulties in managing the solid wastes of around 400 MT generated per day.

At present the Corporation has proposed to install modern bio-methanation plants to convert biodegradable waste, including vegetables and food materials, into power at various places of the city. The six major places identified for the installation of bio-methanation cum power generation plants are at Kakayan burial ground on the Court Road Colony (Ward 12) with 10 tons per day capacity at a cost of Rs. 1.60 crore near Kuppai Medu on Erumapalayam Main Road (Ward 44s) with 10 tons per day capacity at a cost of Rs. 1.60 crore, five tonne capacity plant at Shevapet burial ground (Ward 28) at a cost of Rs. 90 lakh, in Kitchipalayam, Kondalampaaty and Seelnaickampatty. Hence, the project would help in utilizing the waste and generating electricity. Senior officials in the municipal corporation told that about 15,000 watts of electricity could be generated from the waste in all the three plants.

3.8 Legal Framework of the Salem Municipal Solid Waste Management

Swacch Bharat Mission (Urban)

One of the major objectives of Swacch Bharat Mission (Urban) is to improve the efficiency of solid waste management. It aimed to attain 100 percent door to door waste collection and to recover energy from waste. In Tamil Nadu, under this scheme, 100 percent door to door collection was achieved in 11,279 wards in Tamil Nadu. As a part of the programme, Salem Corporation has attempted to set up dry waste collection centres across the city. The first centre in this regard was set up in ward 14 in Hashampatti.

Under the Swacch Survekshan Ranking, 2018, Salem Corporation has obtained 135th rank among the different corporations in India. The low rank was due to the absence of modern scientific municipal solid waste management system. The absence of waste segregation was attributed as the major reason for our low efficiency in solid waste management. Since 40 percent of the total wastes generated in the corporation were dry, it was attempted to set up dry waste collection centres at various places. The residents were sensitised to segregate their dry waste at source and hand it over to the agents. Despite the numerous efforts taken by the Corporation, due to the failure of modern and scientific solid waste management system, Salem Corporation has obtained only 242nd rank with a score of 1888.43 in 2019.

Municipal Solid Wastes (Management and Handling) Rules, 2000

These rules shall apply to every municipal authority responsible for collection, segregation, storage, transportation, processing and disposal of municipal solid wastes.

Responsibility of Municipal Authority

1. Every municipal authority shall, within the territorial area of the municipality, be responsible for the implementation of the provisions of these rules, and for any infrastructure development for the collection, storage, segregation, transportation, processing and disposal of municipal solid wastes.
2. The municipal authority or an operator of a facility shall make an application for the grant of authorization for setting up waste processing and disposal facility including landfills from the State Board or the Committee in order to comply with the norms.
3. The municipal authority shall comply with these rules as per the implementation schedule.
4. The municipal authority shall furnish its annual report,
    a. to the Secretary-in charge of the Department of Urban Development of the concerned State or the case may be of the Union territory, in case of a metropolitan city; or
    b. to the District Magistrate or the Deputy Commissioner concerned in case of all other towns and cities with a copy to the State Board or the Committee on or before the 30th day of June every year.

New Solid Waste Management Rules 2016

The New Solid Waste Management Rules 2016 was given by the Union Ministry of Environment, Forests and Climate Change, by replacing the Municipal Solid Waste (Management and Handling) Rules, 2000. The major amendments of the rule include the following provisions:

- The new rules have mandated the segregation of waste at source to enable the further processes viz. recovery, reuse and recycle. It has become mandatory to segregate the waste into three categories viz. biodegradables, dry and domestic hazardous waste.

- The power to fix the user fee has been given to local bodies for the collection, disposal and processing of wastes from bulk generators. The fee charged by local bodies includes two major categories viz. 'User Fee', the amount have to be paid by generator to waste collector and 'Spot Fine' which will be charged for littering and non-segregation of waste.
- The informal sector in the waste management includes waste pickers and rag pickers and is attempted to be integrated with the formal sector.
- Regarding the management of bio-degradable waste, it was directed to be processed, treated and disposed through composting and bio-methanation as far as possible. The powers to collect the residual waste to the waste collectors can be entrusted with the local bodies.
- Regarding the sale of the compost obtained from the bio-methanation plant, by obtaining the market development assistance from the Department of Fertilizers under the Ministry of Chemicals and Fertilizers, the compost can be sold to the fertilizer companies.
- In order to monitor the implementation of the rules, a Central Monitoring Committee was constituted under the chairmanship of the Secretary, Ministry of Environment and Forests comprising the stakeholders from the Central and State Governments.

As a critique, Solid Waste Management Rules 2016 was found to diminish the scope for decentralised mechanism for solid waste management. A massive awareness campaign was a need of the hour by involving the role of NGOs, students and other communities for the better implementation of the rules.

Plastic Waste Management (Amendment) Rules 2018

This rule has been notified by the Ministry of Environment, Forest and Climate Change on March 27th, 2018. This was an amendment of the Plastic Waste Management rules 2016 and Solid Waste Management rules 2016. The amended rules aimed at the phasing out of multilayered plastics (MLPs). The non-recyclable and non-energy recoverable plastics have also been brought under the category of MLP. The central registration system was prescribed for the registration of the producer/importer/brand owner of plastic products under the amendment. The task of central registration was entrusted with the central pollution control board (CPCB). Regarding small producers/brand owners, the State level registration was prescribed, provided they are operating within one or two States. As a major amendment, explicit pricing of carry bags has been omitted under this act.

A ban on One Time Use and Throw away Plastics by Tamil Nadu Government

In the G.O No. 84 passed on 25.06.2018, under the Environment Protection Act, 1986, Tamil Nadu Government with the view to make Tamil Nadu Plastic free, has banned the manufacture, storage, sale and use of throw away plastics from January 2019 onwards. Under this provision the items banned include plastic carry bags, plastic sheets, plastic tumblers, flags, water pouches and packets. The task of prevention of storage, supply, sale, distribution and consumption was entrusted to the Municipal Corporation Commissioner and District Collector. The exercise of control on manufacturing of plastic items was entrusted with the District Environmental Engineers.

It is noted that the municipal solid waste has been the major concern for the local bodies not only in India but also in all the countries. Every country has been taking various measures to control the solid waste generation. However, the method followed by various countries is found to be different from one to another. Solid Waste Management has been essential for the provision of sanitary and health care to the citizens of every Municipal Corporations. By the field observation it was found that the segregation of waste was inadequate and inefficient in Salem Corporation. The improper maintenance of vehicles involved in the collection of wastes and absence of time schedule for the collection and disposal of wastes were observed in the study area. The steps taken by Salem Corporation in the management of municipal solid waste were found inadequate and unscientific.

4

Economic Analysis of Household Waste Generation, Disposal and Management

The present study has been undertaken to analyze the economics of municipal solid waste management in Salem Corporation. In this regard, analysis has been divided into three parts. The first part of the analysis deals with the generation and disposal of solid waste by the residents of Salem Municipal Corporation. For this purpose, 385 households have been selected out of the families living within the Salem Municipal Corporation limits. The total quantity of solid waste generated in their houses, the method of disposal followed, performance of corporation regarding solid waste management, perceived causes of diseases, willingness to pay for solid waste management, etc. have been discussed in this chapter.

4.1 Household Solid Waste Generation

The quantity of solid waste generated in the house has been measured in terms of grams per day. The solid waste generated has been broadly classified as bio-degradable solid waste, non bio-degradable solid waste and domestic hazardous waste. The quantity of solid waste generated has been divided into five groups – less than 250 gms as very low; 251 to 500 gms as low; 501 to 750 gms as medium; 751 to 1000 gms as high; and more than 1000 gms as very high. The solid waste generated in houses has been analyzed in the dimensions of zone, monthly income, qualification and occupation.

Table 4.1: Solid Waste Generated in Different Zones

Zone	*N*	*Mean*	*Std. Deviation*	*Minimum*	*Maximum*
Hasthampatti	88	673.86	277.263	250	1510
Ammapet	104	474.33	206.453	250	1250
Kondalampatti	82	525.98	182.587	250	1000
Suramangalam	111	542.79	204.593	250	1000
Total	**385**				

Source: Compiled with Primary Data

Table 4.1 shows that the average solid waste generated by the households of Hasthampatti zone was found to be 673. 86 grams per day, while the average solid waste generated by the households of Ammapet zone has been ascertained to be 473.33 grams per day. The average solid waste generated by the households of Kondalampatti region was found to be 525.98 grams per day and that of Suramangalam region has been computed to be 542.79. It denotes that the highest average solid waste has been generated by the households of Hasthampatti zone and the lowest average solid waste has been generated by the households of Suramangalam zone.

The levels of solid wastes generated by the households of the four zones have been presented in the following table:

Table 4.2: Zone and Level of Solid Waste Generated – Two Way Table

Zone	Frequency	Very Low	Low	Medium	High	Very High	Total
Hasthampatti	No.	3	48	14	14	9	88
	%	3.40%	54.50%	15.90%	15.90%	10.20%	100.00%
Ammapet	No.	29	63	5	2	5	104
	%	27.90%	60.60%	4.80%	1.90%	4.80%	100.00%
Kondalampatti	No.	13	48	16	5	0	82
	%	15.90%	58.50%	19.50%	6.10%	0.00%	100.00%
Suramangalam	No.	15	74	9	2	11	111
	%	13.50%	66.70%	8.10%	1.80%	9.90%	100.00%
Total		**60**	**233**	**44**	**23**	**25**	**385**

Source: Compiled with Primary Data

According to the Table 4.2, the majority households (60.51 percent) revealed that they discharge low quantity of solid waste followed by a very low category (15. 58 percent). Among the category of households discharging very high quantity of solid waste, 44 percent were found in the Suramangalam zone.

Out of the 88 households of Hasthampatti zone, 3.4 percent have generated very low level of solid waste whereas 54.5 percent of these households have generated low level of solid waste and 15.9 percent of them have generated medium level of solid waste. High level of solid waste has been generated by 15.9 percent of the households of this zone and very high level of solid waste has been generated by 9 households.

It is observed that among 104 households of Ammapet zone, a very low level of solid waste has been generated by 27.9 percent of them while, low level of solid waste has been generated by 60.6 percent of these households and medium level of solid waste has been generated by 4.8 percent of them. The solid waste generated by 1.9 percent of households has been found to be high whereas the solid waste generated by 4.8 percent of the households of this region has been found to be very high.

Among the households of Kondalampatti very low level of solid waste has been generated by 15.9 percent of them while low level of solid waste has been generated by 58.5 percent of households and medium level of solid waste has been generated by 19.5 percent of them. High level of solid waste has been generated by 6.1 percent of the households of this zone and a very high level of solid waste has been generated by none of them.

The results indicate that the solid waste generated by 13.5 percent of the households of Hasthampatti zone has been found to be very low whereas the solid waste generated by 66.7 percent of them has been reported to be low and the level of solid waste generated by 8.1 percent of them has been found to be medium. The proportion of households of this zone generated high level of solid waste has been found to be 1.8 percent and that of very high level has been ascertained to be 9.9 per cent.

In all the four zones, the highest proportion of households has generated low level of solid waste. However, the lowest proportion of households of Hasthampatti zone has generated very low level of solid waste whereas the lowest portion of households of Ammapet zone has generated high level of solid waste and none of the households of Kondalampatti zone has generated very high level of solid waste. The level of solid waste generated by the lowest proportion of households of Suramangalam zone has been found to be high. It implies that there has been variation in the levels of solid waste generated by the households of the four zones of Salem Corporation.

With a view to understand the significance of variation in the solid waste generated by the households of the four zones, the following hypotheses have been framed and tested:

Null Hypothesis H_0: There is no significant variation in the levels of solid waste generated by the households of four zones of Salem Corporation.

Alternative Hypothesis H_1: There is a significant variation in the levels of solid waste generated by the households of four zones of Salem Corporation.

Table 4.3: Zone and Level of Solid Waste Generated – Anova

Source of variation	*Sum of Squares*	*DF*	*Mean Square*	*F value*	*p value*	*Result*
Between Groups	31.823	3	10.608	11.209	0.000	Rejected**
Within Groups	360.541	381	0.946			
Total	392.364	384				

It could be understood from the Table 4.3 that the F value stating the relationship between the quantities of solid waste generated and the zone in which the households are residing has been found to be 11.209 and the p value was 0.000. Since the p value is less than 0.01, it falls in the rejection region. Hence, the null hypothesis is rejected and the alternative hypothesis is accepted. The hypothesis that 'there is no significant relationship between zone and the level of solid waste generated' does not hold good. It denotes that the level of solid waste generated by the households of Salem Corporation varies from one zone to another. Thus there exists significant difference in the quantum of solid waste generated between the four zones. There exists vast a variations in the size of population, number of commercial and industrial establishments among the four zones in Salem Corporation. Regarding the size of the geographical area also there exists differences among the zones.

Table 4.4: Monthly Income and Solid Waste Generated

Monthly Income	*N*	*Mean*	*Std. Deviation*	*Minimum*	*Maximum*
Less than Rs. 5000	145	427.79	152.514	250	1000
Rs. 5001 to Rs. 10000	122	529.34	164.471	250	1000
Rs. 10001 to Rs. 15000	72	636.81	191.487	500	1000
Rs. 15001 to Rs. 20000	32	758.44	266.12	500	1500
More than Rs. 20000	14	1091.43	233.035	750	1510
Total	385				

Source: Compiled with Primary Data

From the Table 4.4, it is evinced that the average solid waste generated by the households earning a monthly income of less than Rs.5000 has been ascertained to be 427.79 grams per day and that of households in the monthly income group of 'Rs.5001 to Rs.10000' was found to be 529.34 grams per day. In the case of households belonging to the monthly income group of 'Rs.10001 to Rs.15000', the average solid waste generated was found to be 636.81 grams per day and the reported average solid waste generated by the households earning a monthly income of 'Rs.15001 to Rs.20000' has been found to be 758.44 grams per day. On an average, 1091.43 grams per day solid waste has been generated by the households pertaining to the monthly income group of 'more than Rs.20000'.

Table 4.5: Monthly Income and Level of Solid Waste Generated – Two Way Table

Monthly Income	Frequency	Very Low	Low	Medium	High	Very High	Total
Less than Rs.5000	No.	46	95	0	4	0	145
	%	31.70%	65.50%	0.00%	2.80%	0.00%	100.00%
Rs.5001 to Rs.10000	No.	14	81	20	2	5	122
	%	11.50%	66.40%	16.40%	1.60%	4.10%	100.00%
Rs.10001 to Rs.15000	No.	0	43	17	9	3	72
	%	0.00%	59.70%	23.60%	12.50%	4.20%	100.00%
Rs.15001 to Rs.20000	No.	0	14	5	6	7	32
	%	0.00%	43.80%	15.60%	18.80%	21.90%	100.00%
More than Rs.20000	No.	0	0	2	2	10	14
	%	0.00%	0.00%	14.30%	14.30%	71.40%	100.00%
Total		**60**	**233**	**44**	**23**	**25**	**385**

Source: Compiled with Primary Data

Among the category of low waste generators, a majority was in the low income category of less than 5000 per month. This reveals that, lower the income, less will be the consumption and subsequently less quantity of waste will be disposed by them. Similarly among the category of high waste generators, a majority are earning more than Rs. 20000 per month.

A very low level of solid waste has been generated by 31.7 percent of the households earning a monthly income of 'Less than Rs.5000' while low level of solid waste has been generated by 65.5 percent of these households and medium level of solid waste has been generated by none of them. High level of solid waste has been found to be generated by 2.8 percent of the households belonging to this category and a very high level of solid waste has been generated by none of them.

It is observed that a very low level of solid waste has been generated by 11.5 percent of the respondents earning a monthly income of 'Rs.5001 to Rs.10000' while low level of solid waste has been generated by 66.4 percent of these respondents and medium level of solid waste has been generated by 16.4 percent of them. A High level of solid waste has been found to be generated by 1.6 percent of the respondents belonging to this category and a very high level of solid waste has been generated by 4.1 percent of them.

The results showed that a very low level of solid waste has been generated by none of the households earning a monthly income of 'Rs.10001 to Rs.15000' while a low level of solid waste has been generated by 59.7 percent of these households and a medium level of solid waste has been generated by 23.6 percent of them. A High level of solid waste has been found to be generated by 12.5 percent of the households belonging to this category and a very high level of solid waste has been generated by 4.2 percent of them.

The analysis of monthly income and level of solid waste generated revealed that a very low level of solid waste has been generated by none of the households earning a monthly income of 'Rs.15001 to Rs.20000' while a low level of solid waste has been generated by 43.8 percent of these households and a medium level of solid waste has been generated by 15.6 percent of them. A High level of solid waste has been found to be generated by 18.8 percent of the households belonging to this category and a very high level of solid waste has been generated by 21.9 percent of them.

It is divulged from the analysis that a very low level of solid waste has been generated by none of the households earning a monthly income of 'More than Rs.20000' while a low level of solid waste has been generated by none of these households and a medium level of solid waste has been generated by 14.3 percent of them. A High level of solid waste has been found to be generated by 14.3 percent of the households belonging to this category and a very high level of solid waste has been generated by 71.4 percent of them.

With a view to understand the significance of variation in the solid waste generated by the households of different monthly income groups, the following hypotheses have been framed and tested:

Null Hypothesis H_0: There is no significant variation in the levels of solid waste generated by the households of different monthly income groups of Salem Corporation.

Alternative Hypothesis H_1: There is a significant variation in the levels of solid waste generated by the households of different monthly income groups of Salem Corporation.

Table 4.6: Monthly Income and Level of Solid Waste Generated – Anova

Source of variation	*Sum of Squares*	*DF*	*Mean Square*	*F value*	*p value*	*Result*
Between Groups	151.031	4	37.758	59.453	0.000	Rejected**
Within Groups	241.333	380	0.635			
Total	**392.364**	**384**				

Table 4.6 proclaims that the F value stating the relationship between the levels of solid waste generated and the monthly income of households has been found to be 59.453 and the p value was 0.000. Since the p value is less than 0.01, it falls in the rejection region. Hence, the null hypothesis is rejected and the alternative hypothesis

is accepted. The hypothesis that 'there is no significant relationship between monthly income and the level of solid waste generated' does not hold good. It denotes that the level of solid waste generated by the residents of Salem Corporation varies in accordance with their monthly income. There exists a significant differences in the quantum of solid waste generated by households with different levels of income. Households earning higher income, generate higher quantum of waste and vice versa as found in previous studies (Medina M, 1997 & Amina Zia et.al 2017).

Table 4.7: Educational Level and Solid Waste Generated

Educational Level	*N*	*Mean*	*Std. Deviation*	*Minimum*	*Maximum*
Illiterates	155	440.71	150.829	250	1000
School Level	63	469.52	159.368	250	1000
Graduation	73	596.44	174.749	250	1000
Post Graduation and above	94	750.85	272.309	500	1510
Total	**385**				

Source: Compiled with Primary Data

Educational standard of the household head plays a significant role in determining their attitude towards the generation of wastes. From the Table 4.7, it is evinced that the average solid waste generated by the illiterate respondents has been ascertained to be 440.71 grams per day and that of respondents educated up to school level was found to be 469.52 grams per day. In the case of respondents having graduate level education, the average solid waste generated was found to be 596.44 grams per day and the reported average solid waste generated by the respondents having qualified post graduation and above have been found to be 750.85 grams per day.

Table 4.8: Educational Level and Level of Solid Waste Generated – Two way table

Educational Level	Frequency	Very Low	Low	Medium	High	Very High	Total
Illiterates	No.	44	103	4	4	0	155
	%	28.40%	66.50%	2.60%	2.60%	0.00%	100.00%
School Level	No.	14	42	4	1	2	63
	%	22.20%	66.70%	6.30%	1.60%	3.20%	100.00%
Graduation	No.	2	46	17	4	4	73
	%	2.70%	63.00%	23.30%	5.50%	5.50%	100.00%
Post Graduation and above	No.	0	42	19	14	19	94
	%	0.00%	44.70%	20.20%	14.90%	20.20%	100.00%
Total		**60**	**233**	**44**	**23**	**25**	**385**

Source: Compiled with Primary Data

Among the category of low waste generators, a majority were illiterates, which implies that the education is not a barrier in determining the attitude of a person towards waste generation. Among the category of high and a very high waste generator, a majority were qualified with higher level of education as graduates and post graduates.

Table 4.8 divulges that a very low level of solid waste has been generated by 28.4 percent of the illiterate household heads while a low level of solid waste has been generated by 66.5 percent of this category and a medium level of solid waste has been generated by 2.6 percent of them. A High level of solid waste has been found to be generated by 2.6 percent of the respondents belonging to this category and a very high level of solid waste has been generated by none of them.

It is observed that a very low level of solid waste has been generated by 22.2 percent of the respondents having school level education while a low level of solid waste has been generated by 66.7 percent of these respondents and a medium level of solid waste has been generated by 6.3 percent of them. A High level of solid waste has been found to be generated by 1.6 percent of the respondents belonging to this category and a very high level of solid waste has been generated by 3.2 percent of them.

The results showed that a very low level of solid waste has been generated by 2.7 percent of the graduate respondents while a low level of solid waste has been generated by 63 percent of these respondents and a medium level of solid waste has been generated by 23.3 percent of them. A High level of solid waste has been found to be generated by 5.5 percent of the respondents belonging to this category and very a high level of solid waste has been generated by 5.5 percent of them.

The analysis of educational level and the level of solid waste generated revealed that a very low level of solid waste has been generated by none of the respondents having qualified post graduation and above, while a low level of solid waste has been generated by 44.7 percent of these respondents and a medium level of solid waste has been generated by 20.2 percent of them. A High level of solid waste has been found to be generated by 14.9 percent of the respondents belonging to this category and a very high level of solid waste has been generated by 20.2 percent of them.

With a view to understand the significance of variation in the solid waste generated by the household heads with different levels of education, the following hypotheses have been framed and tested:

Null Hypothesis H_0: There is no significant variation in the quantity of solid waste generated by the respondents with different educational standards.

Alternative Hypothesis H_1: There is a significant variation in the quantity of solid waste generated by the respondents with different educational standards.

Table 4.9: Educational Level and Level of Solid Waste Generated – Anova

Source of variation	*Sum of Squares*	*DF*	*Mean Square*	*F value*	*p value*	*Result*
Between Groups	109.878	3	36.626	49.399	0.000	Rejected**
Within Groups	282.485	381	0.741			
Total	**392.364**	**384**				

It could be understood from the Table 4.9 that the F value stating the relationship between the levels of solid waste generated and the educational level of the respondents has been found to be 49.399 and the p value was 0.000. Since the p value is less than 0.01, it falls in the rejection region. Hence, the null hypothesis is rejected and the alternative hypothesis is accepted. The hypothesis that 'there is no significant relationship between educational level and the level of solid waste generated' does not hold good. It denotes that the level of solid waste generated by the households of Salem Corporation varies in accordance with their educational levels. The significant difference was found in the quantity of waste generated between the different educational standards of the household heads.

Table 4.10: Duncan's Multiple Range Test for Comparison of Waste Generation between the Levels of Education

Educational Qualification	N	Subset for alpha = 0.05			
		1	2	3	4
Illiterates	155	1.0903			
School Level	63		1.2222		
Graduation	73			1.8493	
Post Graduation and Above	94				2.2447
Sig.		1.000	1.000	1.000	1.000

The one way ANOVA was used to test the impact of different levels of education on generation of waste. The p value <0.001 revealed the significant difference between the quantity of waste generated by household heads having different levels of education. The Duncan's test further reveals that the household heads who qualified higher standard of education as graduation and post graduation and above generates huge quantum of waste. Due to their higher level of education, they avail higher income earning opportunities than poorly educated heads. Due to their higher income they consume and dispose more.

Table 4.11: Occupational Status and Solid Waste Generated

Occupational Status	*N*	*Mean*	*Std. Deviation*	*Minimum*	*Maximum*
Coolie	171	441.87	144.161	250	1000
Farmers	47	475.11	183.064	250	1000
Business	52	813.65	288.601	500	1510
Employees	80	600.5	175.909	250	1000
Profession	35	679.14	239.452	500	1250
Total	**385**				

Source: Compiled with Primary Data

From the Table 4.11, it is evinced that the average solid waste generated by household heads occupied as coolies has been ascertained to be 441.87 grams per day and that of farmers was found to be 475.11 grams per day. In the case of business occupation the average solid waste generated was found to be 813.65 grams per day and the reported average solid waste generated by the employee category has been found to be 600.5 grams per day. On an average, 679.14 grams per day solid waste has been generated by the household heads as professionals.

Table 4.12: Occupational Status and Level of Solid Waste Generated – Two Way Table

Occupational Status	Frequency	Very Low	Low	Medium	High	Very High	Total
Coolie	No.	46	118	3	4	0	171
	%	26.90%	69.00%	1.80%	2.30%	0.00%	100.00%
Farmers	No.	12	26	5	2	2	47
	%	25.50%	55.30%	10.60%	4.30%	4.30%	100.00%
Business	No.	0	18	9	11	14	52
	%	0.00%	34.60%	17.30%	21.20%	26.90%	100.00%
Employees	No.	2	52	19	2	5	80
	%	2.50%	65.00%	23.80%	2.50%	6.30%	100.00%
Profession	No.	0	19	8	4	4	35
	%	0.00%	54.30%	22.90%	11.40%	11.40%	100.00%
Total		**60**	**233**	**44**	**23**	**25**	**385**

Source: Compiled with Primary Data

Among the low income category, a majority was occupied as coolies, which implies that due to their low income they generate less quantity of waste. A Majority was engaged in business that generates a high and a very high quantity of waste. Thus occupation plays a significant role in determining the quantity of waste generated by them.

It is evident from the Table 4.12 that a very low level of solid waste has been generated by 26.9 percent of the coolie respondents while a low level of solid waste has been generated by 69 percent of these respondents and a medium level of solid waste has been generated by 1.8 percent of them. A High level of solid waste has been found to be generated by 2.3 percent of the respondents belonging to this category and a very high level of solid waste has been generated by none of them.

It is observed that a very low level of solid waste has been generated by 25.5 percent of the respondents engaged in farming activities. While a low level of solid waste has been generated by 55.3 percent of these respondents and a medium level of solid waste has been generated by 10.6 percent of them. A High level of solid waste has been found to be generated by 4.3 percent of the respondents belonging to this category and a very high level of solid waste has been generated by 4.3 percent of them.

The results showed that a very low level of solid waste has been generated by none of the household heads who were engaged in business while a low level of solid waste has been generated by 34.6 percent of these respondents and a medium level of solid waste has been generated by 17.3 percent of them. A High level of solid waste has been found to be generated by 21.2 percent of the respondents belonging to this category and a very high level of solid waste has been generated by 26.9 percent of them.

The analysis of occupation and the level of solid waste generated revealed that a very low level of solid waste has been generated by 2.5 percent of the employee category of respondents while a low level of solid waste has been generated by 65 percent of these respondents and a medium level of solid waste has been generated by 23.8 percent of them. A High level of solid waste has been found to be generated by 2.5 percent of the respondents belonging to this category and a very high level of solid waste has been generated by 6.3 percent of them.

It is realized from the analysis that a very low level of solid waste has been generated by none of the respondents occupied as professionals while a low level of solid waste has been generated by 54.3 percent of these respondents and a medium level of solid waste has been generated by 22.9 percent of them. A High level of solid waste has been found to be generated by 11.4 percent of the respondents belonging to this category and a very high level of solid waste has been generated by 11.4 percent of them.

With a view to understand the significance of variation in the solid waste generated by the household heads who are occupied at different nature of work, the following hypotheses have been framed and tested:

Null Hypothesis H_0: There is no significant variation in the levels of solid waste generated by the household heads, occupied at different nature of work.

Alternative Hypothesis H_1: There is no significant variation in the levels of solid waste generated by the household heads, occupied at different nature of work.

Table 4.13: Occupational Status and Level of Solid Waste Generated – Anova

Source of variation	*Sum of Squares*	*DF*	*Mean Square*	*F value*	*p value*	*Result*
Between Groups	119.8	4	29.95	41.755	0.000	Rejected**
Within Groups	272.564	380	0.717			
Total	**392.364**	**384**				

According to the Table 4.13 the F value stating the relationship between the levels of solid waste generated and the occupational status of the respondents has been found to be 41.755 and the p value was 0.000. Since the p value is less than 0.01, it falls in the rejection region. Hence, the null hypothesis is rejected and the alternative hypothesis is accepted. The hypothesis that 'there is no significant relationship between the occupational status and the level of solid waste generated' does not hold good. It denotes that the level of solid waste generated by the households of Salem Corporation varies in accordance with the occupational status of the household heads.

Table 4.14: Duncan's Multiple Range Test for Comparison of Waste Between the Types of Occupation

Occupation	N	Subset for alpha = 0.05				
		1	2	3	4	5
Coolie	179	1.0726				
Farmers	49		1.3673			
Employees	82			1.8293		
Profession	37				2.1351	
Business	53					2.3962
Sig.		1.000	1.000	1.000	1.000	1.000

The one way ANOVA was used to test the impact of different occupations on generation of waste. The p value <0.001 revealed the significant difference between the quantity of waste generated by different group of occupations. The Duncan's test further reveals that among the different categories of occupations, professionals and business people generate huge quantum of waste. The higher income earned by the category of the above said group attributed their higher waste generation, since they have more financial ability to buy more goods. Consequently their quantum of waste generation and disposal also increases.

4.2 Factors affecting the Waste Generation

To investigate the factors affecting the total solid waste generated by households multiple regression analysis has been used.

The following explanatory variables have been selected to determine the quantity of waste generation based on the previous studies.

Table 4.15: Description of Explanatory Variables

Variable	Description	Unit of Measurement	Expected Sign
Income	Total Average Monthly Income of the Household	1 = < 5000 2 = 5001 – 10000 3 = 10001 – 15000 4 = 15001 – 20000 5 = >20001	+
Education	Level of Education attained by the Household Head	1 = Illiterate 2 = School Level 3 = Graduation 4 = Post Graduation and above	+
Family Size	Total Number of Members currently residing in the house	Number of Individuals	+
Personal Attitude	Attitude towards segregation and reuse of solid waste	1 = Yes 2 = No	+

Household income is expected to have a significant positive relationship with the quantity of waste generation based on various previous studies (Rafia Afroz, et. al 2010 and Pham Thi Thuy Trang et. al., 2016). It implies that when income increases consumption also increases, which finally increases the quantity of waste. Thus income is expected to positively influence the quantity of waste generated by households.

Higher the educational qualification, greater will be the job opportunities and income generation, which will subsequently increase their consumption and waste generation. Due to their change in life style, they tend to generate more waste. With the support of previous studies, the present study also expected that education will have a positive impact on the quantity of waste generated (Bijan Maskey and Mrinila Singh, 2017).

Larger the size of family more will be the consumption and consequently more will be waste generation. Thus family size is expected to have a positive relationship with the quantity of waste generated. Previous studies have also found the positive relationship between household size and quantity of waste generation (Nilanthi J G J Bandara et al., 2007).

The personal attitude of the households towards the segregation and reuse of waste plays a significant role in determining the amount of waste generated. If the households attempt to segregate and reuse their waste, then their quantity of waste generated will be automatically reduced and vice versa. Thus the present study has assigned positive sign for relationship between personal attitude towards segregation and reuse of waste and quantity of waste generation. The past studies done by (Muhdin Muhammedhussen Batu et al., 2016) have also assumed the same.

Table 4.16 : Summary of Selected Variables used in the Regression Model

Personal Attitude towards Segregation and Reuse of Waste	*Observation (Percentage)*
Yes	184 (47.8)
No	201 (52.2)
Total	385

Of the 385 sample households, 52.2 percent have failed to segregate and reuse their waste. Around 47.8 percent have attempted to segregate and reuse their waste.

Table 4.17: Model Summary

Model	R	R Square	Adjusted R Square	Std. Error of the Estimate	Durbin-Watson
1	.860[a]	.739	.736	.32484	1.896

The co-efficient of correlation between dependent variable (total waste generated) and the independent variables (income, educational qualification, family size and personal attitude towards waste segregation and disposal) has been found to be 0.860. The value of R-square is 0.739, which indicates that 73.1 percent of the changes in the total waste generated have been influenced by the independent variables. The durbin Watson statistic is 1.896, which implies that the data is not auto correlated.

Table 4.18: Anova

Source of variation	Sum of Squares	DF	Mean Square	F value	p value	Result
Regression	113.606	4	28.401	269.155	.000[b]	
Residual	40.098	380	.106			
Total	153.704	384				

The above ANOVA table proved the significant relationship between total waste generated and its determinants with its significant value of less than 0.001. The F value of 269.155, significant at one percent indicates that the regression model is best fit.

Table 4.19: Regression Co-Efficients

Variables	Unstandardized Coefficients		Standardized Coefficients	T	Sig.
	B	Std. Error	Beta		
(Constant)	.048	.079		.607	.544
Monthly Family Income	.339	.027	.592	12.452	.000
Perception towards Segregation and Reuse of Solid Waste	.242	.037	.192	6.556	.000

Educational Qualification	.085	.025	.165	3.449	.001
Members of the Family	.052	.015	.093	3.458	.001

Dependent Variable: Quantity of Waste Generated.

From the regression model, the variables viz. income, family size, educational qualification and personal attitudes were found significantly related with quantum of waste generation.

The household income is positively related with the quantity of waste generation at one percent level of significance. It implies that when income increases consumption also increases, which finally increases the quantity of waste. The Size of family, educational qualification and personal attitudes towards waste disposal were positively related with the quantity of waste generated at one percent level of significance. Larger the size of family more will be the consumption and quantum of waste generation. Higher the educational qualification, the greater will be the job opportunities and income generation, which will subsequently increase their consumption and waste generation. Due to their change in life style, they tend to generate more waste.

4.3 Disposal of Solid Waste

The solid waste generated has been disposed by the households under different methods. For the purpose of the present study, the method of disposal by households has been classified as burning, disposal at municipal waste bin, road side, canals, etc. and other methods. The zone wise method of disposal by households has been furnished in the following table:

Table 4.20: Zone and Methods of Disposal by Households

Zone	*Frequency*	*Burning*	*Municipal Waste bin*	*Road side, Canals etc.*	*Other Methods*	*Total*
Hasthampatti	No.	1	82	4	1	88
	%	1.10%	93.20%	4.50%	1.10%	100.00%

Ammapet	No.	3	93	8	0	104
	%	2.90%	89.40%	7.70%	0.00%	100.00%
Kondalampatti	No.	1	74	7	0	82
	%	1.20%	90.20%	8.50%	0.00%	100.00%
Suramangalam	No.	2	103	6	0	111
	%	1.80%	92.80%	5.40%	0.00%	100.00%
Total		**7**	**352**	**25**	**1**	**385**

Source: Compiled with Primary Data

Disposing the waste in municipal waste bins was the method of disposal largely followed in Salem Corporation (91.42 percent) followed by discharging at road sides, canals etc (6.49). The strategy of disposing at bins was largely followed in Suramangalam zone (29.26 percent), and Ammapet Zone (26.42).

Table 4.20 divulges that 1.1 percent of the Hasthampatti households have been burning the solid waste while 93.2 percent of them have been disposing of the solid waste through municipal waste and 4.5 percent of these households have been disposing of the solid waste on the road side, canals, etc. The other methods of disposal have been followed by 1.1 percent of households.

The results reveal that 2.9 percent of households in Ammapet zone have been burning the solid waste while 89.4 percent of them have been disposing of the solid waste through municipal waste bins and 7.7 percent of these households have been disposing of their solid waste on the road side, canals, etc.

It is observed from the analysis that 1.2 percent of households in Kondalampatti zone have been burning the solid waste while 90.2 percent of them have been disposing of the solid waste through municipal waste and 8.5 percent of these households have been disposing of the solid waste on the road side, canals, etc.

The analysis of zone wise disposal methods of solid waste indicates that 1.8 percent of households in Suramangalam zone have been burning the solid waste while 92.8 percent of them have been disposing of the solid waste through municipal waste and 5.4 percent of households have been disposing of the solid waste on the road side, canals, etc.

In order to examine the significance of relationship between the methods of disposal of solid waste by households among four zones the following hypotheses have been framed and tested:

Null Hypothesis H_0: There is no significant relationship between the methods of disposal of solid waste by households among four zones.

Alternative Hypothesis H_1: There is a significant relationship between the methods of disposal of solid waste by households among four zones.

Table 4.21: Zone and Methods of Disposal by Households-Chi Square Test

Factor	*Chi square value*	*DF*	*p value*	*Result*
Methods of disposal	5.997	9	0.740	Accepted

Table 4.21 reveals that the chi square value stating the relationship between zone and method of disposal of solid waste followed by households has been found to be 5.997 and the p value was 0.740. Since the p value is greater than 0.05, it falls in the acceptance region. Hence, the null hypothesis is accepted. The hypothesis that 'there is no significant relationship between the zone and method of disposal by households' holds good. It denotes that method of disposal of the solid waste followed by households does not vary with the zone in which they are residing.

4.4 Sorting & Separating Before Disposal

The municipal corporations insist the households to sort and separate the solid waste before disposal in order to collect the degradable and non degradable wastes separately and make the disposal simple. In this regard, the respondents were asked to state whether they have been sorting and separating the solid waste before disposal. The results have been furnished in the following table:

Table 4.22: Zone and Sorting & Separating the Solid Waste Before Disposal

Zone	*Frequency*	*Yes*	*No*	*Total*
Hasthampatti	No.	21	67	88
	%	23.90%	76.10%	100.00%
Ammapet	No.	19	85	104
	%	18.30%	81.70%	100.00%
Kondalampatti	No.	12	70	82
	%	14.60%	85.40%	100.00%
Suramangalam	No.	13	98	111
	%	11.70%	88.30%	100.00%
Total		**184**	**201**	**385**

Source: Compiled with Primary Data

It is made clear from the Table 4.22 that out of 88 households of Hasthampatti zone 23.9 percent of them have been sorting and separating the solid waste before disposal while 76.1 percent of them have not been sorting and separating the solid waste before disposal.

Among 104 households of Ammapet zone 18.3 percent of them have been sorting and separating the solid waste before disposal while 81.7 percent of them have not been sorting and separating the solid waste before disposal.

The results reveal that out of 82 households of Kondalampatti zone 14.6 percent of them have been sorting and separating the solid waste before disposal while 85.4 percent of them have not been sorting and separating the solid waste before disposal.

It is understood from the analysis that out of 111 households of Suramangalam zone 11.7 percent of them have been sorting and separating the solid waste before disposal while 88.3 percent of them have not been sorting and separating the solid waste before disposal.

It envisages that sorting and separating of solid waste have not been made by most of the households cf all the four zones.

In order to examine the significance of relationship between sorting and separating before disposal of solid waste by households among the four zones the following hypotheses have been framed and tested:

Null Hypothesis H_0: There is no significant relationship between sorting and separating before disposal of solid waste by households among the four zones

Alternative Hypothesis H_1: There is a significant relationship between sorting and separating before disposal of solid waste by households among the four zones.

Table 4.23: Zone and Sorting & Separating before Disposal – Chi Square Test

Factor	*Chi square value*	*DF*	*p value*	*Result*
Sorting and Separating before Disposal	5.609	3	0.132	Accepted

According to the Table 4.23 the chi square value stating the relationship between zone and sorting and separating before disposal of solid waste followed by households has been found to be 5.609 and the p value was 0.132. Since the p value is greater than 0.05, it falls in the acceptance region. Hence, the null hypothesis is accepted. The hypothesis that 'there is no significant relationship between sorting and separating before disposal among the four zones holds good. It implies that sorting and separating before disposal did not vary among the households of the four zones of Salem Corporation.

4.5 Frequency of Clearance of Solid Waste

The household heads were asked to state the frequency of clearance of solid waste made in their area by Salem Corporation. In this regard, the frequency has been classified as daily; once in three days; once in week and once in a month. The responses given by the sample respondents have been presented in the following table:

Table 4.24: Zone and Frequency of Clearance of Solid Waste by Corporation

Zone	*Frequency*	*Daily*	*Once in Three Days*	*Once in a Week*	*Once in a Month*	*Total*
Hasthampatti	No.	57	27	3	1	88
	%	64.80%	30.70%	3.40%	1.10%	100.00%
Ammapet	No.	53	47	4	0	104
	%	51.00%	45.20%	3.80%	0.00%	100.00%
Kondalampatti	No.	41	38	3	0	82
	%	50.00%	46.30%	3.70%	0.00%	100.00%
Suramangalam	No.	52	57	1	1	111
	%	46.80%	51.40%	0.90%	0.90%	100.00%
Total		**203**	**169**	**11**	**2**	**385**

Source: Compiled with Primary Data

Around 52.72 percent of households reveal that there was a daily clearance of waste in their area followed by clearance at once in three days (43.86 percent).

From the Table 4.24, it is revealed that the solid waste has been cleared daily as reported by 64.8 percent of the households of Hasthampatti zone while 30.7 percent of them have stated the clearance of solid waste has been made by Salem Corporation once in three days and according to 3.4 percent of households solid waste clearance is made once in a week. It is mentioned by 1.1 percent of them that the solid waste is cleared once in a month.

The solid waste has been cleared daily as reported by 51 percent of the households of Ammapet zone while 45.2 percent of them have stated the clearance of solid waste has been made by Salem Corporation once in three days and according to 3.8 percent of these residents solid waste clearance is made once in a week. It is mentioned by none of them that the solid waste is cleared once in a month.

The results reveal that the solid waste has been cleared daily as reported by 50.0 percent of the households of Kondalampatti zone while 46.3 percent of them have stated the clearance of solid waste has been made by Salem Corporation once in three days and according to 3.7 percent of households solid waste clearance is made once in a week. It is mentioned by none of them that the solid waste is cleared once in a month.

It is understood from the analysis that the solid waste has been cleared daily as reported by 46.8 percent of the households of Suramangalam zone while 51.4 percent of them have stated the clearance of solid waste has been made by Salem Corporation once in three days and according to 0.9 percent of households solid waste clearance is made once in a week. It is mentioned by 0.9 percent of them that the solid waste is cleared once in a month.

In order to examine the significance of relationship between the frequency of clearance of solid waste by Corporation among the four zones the following hypotheses have been framed and tested:

Null Hypothesis H_0: There is no significant relationship between the frequency of clearance of solid waste by Salem Corporation among the four zones.

Alternative Hypothesis H_1: There is a significant relationship between the frequency of clearance of solid waste by Salem Corporation among the four zones.

Table 4.25: Zone and Frequency of Clearance of Solid Waste by Corporation – Chi Square Test

Factor	*Chi square value*	*DF*	*p value*	*Result*
Frequency ofClearance	12.427	9	0.190	Accepted

Table 4.25 proclaims that the chi square value stating the relationship between zone and frequency of clearance of solid waste by Salem Corporation has been found to be 12.427 and the p value was 0.190. Since the p value is greater than 0.05, it falls in the acceptance region. Hence, the null hypothesis is accepted. The hypothesis that 'there

is no significant relationship between the frequency of clearance of solid waste by Salem Corporation among the four zones holds good. It implies that the frequency of clearance of solid waste did not vary in accordance with the households of the four zones of Salem Corporation.

4.6 Performance of Municipal Corporation in Solid Waste Management

The performance of Salem Corporation in solid waste management has been assessed by rating of performance by the household heads as good and bad. The rating made by the sample household heads has been consolidated and presented in the following table:

Table 4.26: Zone and Performance of Municipal Corporation in Solid Waste Management

Zone	*Frequency*	*Good*	*Bad*	*Total*
Hasthampatti	No.	28	60	88
	%	31.80%	68.20%	100.00%
Ammapet	No.	55	49	104
	%	52.90%	47.10%	100.00%
Kondalampatti	No.	49	33	82
	%	59.80%	40.20%	100.00%
Suramangalam	No.	60	51	111
	%	54.10%	45.90%	100.00%
Total		**192**	**193**	**385**

Source: Compiled with Primary Data

Of the 385 sample households roughly equal number of households assessed that the performance of solid waste management by Salem Corporation was good. The remaining half assessed the performance of Corporation as bad. Of the 193, who assessed the performance of Corporation as bad, 31.08 percent were found in Hasthampatti Zone, followed by Suramangalam Zone (26.42 percent). Among the households who assessed the performance of Corporation as good, 31.25 percent were found in Suramangalam Zone, followed by Ammapet Zone (28.64) percent.

Table 4.26 evinces that 68.2 percent of the households of Hasthampatti zone have reported that the performance of the corporation in solid waste management is bad while 31.8 percent of them have stated that the performance of the corporation in solid waste management is good.

It could be understood that 47.1 percent of the households of Ammapet zone have reported that the performance of the corporation in solid waste management is bad while 52.9 percent of them have stated that the performance of the corporation in solid waste management is good.

The analysis of zone and performance of corporation in solid waste management indicates that 40.2 percent of the households of Kondalampatti zone have reported that the performance of the corporation in solid waste management is bad while 59.8 percent of them have stated that the performance of the corporation in solid waste management is good.

The results reveal that 45.9 percent of the households of Suramangalam zone have reported that the performance of the corporation in solid waste management is bad while 54.1 percent of them have stated that the performance of the corporation in solid waste management is good.

In order to examine the significance of relationship between the performance of corporation in solid waste management among four zones the following hypotheses have been framed and tested:

Null Hypothesis H_0: There is no significant relationship between the performances of Salem Corporation in solid waste management among the four zones.

Alternative Hypothesis H_1: There is a significant relationship between the performances of Salem Corporation in solid waste management among the four zones.

Table 4.27: Zone and Performance of Municipal Corporation in Solid Waste Management – Chi Square Test

Factor	*Chi square value*	*DF*	*p value*	*Result*
Performance of Municipal Corporation	15.832	3	0.001	Rejected **

It could be realized from the Table 4.27 that the chi square value stating the relationship between the performance of Salem Corporation in solid waste management among the four zones has been found to be 15.832 and the p value was 0.001. Since the p value is less than 0.01, it falls in the rejection region. Hence, the null hypothesis is rejected and the alternative hypothesis is accepted. The hypothesis that 'there is no significant relationship between the performance of Salem Corporation in solid waste management among the four zones does not hold good. It implies that the performance of Salem Corporation in solid waste management varied in the four zones of Salem Corporation as indicated by the households.

4.7 Methods of Collection and Disposal of Solid Waste by Corporation

The solid waste generated and disposed by the households has been collected and disposed by Salem Corporation using different methods. For the purpose of the present study, the methods of collection and disposal of solid waste by Salem Corporation have been categorized as hand carts, lorries, tractors, bullock carts and tricycles. The following table shows the zone wise methods of collection and disposal of solid waste by Salem Corporation.

Table 4.28: Zone wise Methods of Collection and Disposal of Solid Waste by Salem Corporation

Zone	*Frequency*	*Hand Cart*	*Lorry*	*Tractor*	*Bullock Cart*	*Tricycle*	*Total*
Hasthampatti	No.	7	5	12	0	64	88
	%	8.00%	5.70%	13.60%	0.00%	72.70%	100.00%
Ammapet	No.	12	39	8	12	33	104
	%	11.50%	37.50%	7.70%	11.50%	31.70%	100.00%
Kondalampatti	No.	2	4	15	5	56	82
	%	2.40%	4.90%	18.30%	6.10%	68.30%	100.00%
Suramangalam	No.	22	12	18	2	57	111
	%	19.80%	10.80%	16.20%	1.80%	51.40%	100.00%
Total		**43**	**60**	**53**	**19**	**210**	**385**

Source: Compiled with Primary Data

Tricycles (54.54 percent) were the major mode of collection and disposal in Salem Corporation, which was largely used in Hasthampatti Zone followed by Suramangalam Zone.

According to Table 4.28, in Hasthampatti zone 8 percent of households have reported that the solid waste has been collected and disposed by hand cart whereas 5.7 percent of these households have stated that the lorry has been used for collection and disposal of solid waste and 13.6 percent of them have mentioned that the solid waste has been collected and disposed by tractor. Bullock cart has been used for collection and disposal of solid waste as indicated by none of the households and tricycle has been used for collection and disposal of solid waste according to 72.7 percent of them.

Among the househoLdss of Ammapet zone, 11.5 percent of them have reported that solid waste has been collected and disposed by hand cart whereas 37.5 percent of these households have stated that the lorry has been used for collection and disposal of solid waste and 7.7 percent of them have mentioned that the solid waste has been collected and disposed by tractor. Bullock cart has been used for collection and disposal of solid waste as indicated by 11.5 percent of households and tricycle has been used for collection and disposal of solid waste according to 31.7 percent of them.

It is realized that 2.4 percent of the households of Kondalampatti zone have reported that solid waste has been collected and disposed by hand cart whereas 4.9 percent of households have stated that lorry has been used for collection and disposal of solid waste and 18.3 percent of them have mentioned that the solid waste has been collected and disposed by tractor. Bullock cart has been used for collection and disposal of solid waste as indicated by 6.1 percent of households and tricycle has been used for collection and disposal of solid waste according to 68.3 percent of them.

The results indicate that in Suramangalam Zone, 19.8 percent households have reported that solid waste has been collected and disposed by hand cart whereas 10.8 percent of the households have stated that the lorry has been used for collection and disposal of solid waste and 16.2 percent of them have mentioned that the solid waste has been collected and disposed by tractor. Bullock cart has been used for collection and disposal of solid waste as indicated by 1.8 percent of the households and tricycle has been used for collection and disposal of solid waste according to 51.4 percent of them.

In order to examine the significance of relationship between the methods of collection and disposal of solid waste among the four zones the following hypotheses have been framed and tested:

Null Hypothesis H_0: There is no significant relationship between the methods of collection and disposal of solid waste among the four zones.

Alternative Hypothesis H_1: There is a significant relationship between the methods of collection and disposal of solid waste among the four zones.

Table 4.29: Zone and Methods of Collection and Disposal of Solid Waste by Corporation – Anova

Source of variation	*Sum of squares*	*DF*	*Mean Square*	*F value*	*p value*	*Result*
Between Groups	91.513	3	30.504	14.967	0.000	Rejected**
Within Groups	776.502	381	2.038			
Total	**868.016**	**384**				

According to the Table 4.29 the chi square value stating the relationship between methods of collection and disposal of solid waste among the four zones has been found to be 14.967 and the p value was 0.000. Since the p value is less than 0.01, it falls in the rejection region. Hence, the null hypothesis is rejected and the alternative hypothesis is accepted. The hypothesis that 'there is no significant relationship between the methods of collection and disposal of solid waste among the four zones does not hold good. It implies that the methods of collection and disposal of solid waste varied from one zone to another.

4.8 Signs & Symptoms and Diseases

It is considered that the households would have been suffering from signs and symptoms or diseases. In this regard, the respondents were asked to state whether their family members have been affected by signs and symptoms or diseases. Signs and symptoms include cough and cold, fever, headache, diarrhea, skin infection and eye irritation. Diseases include cholera, jaundice, typhoid, dengue fever, rat fever, chicken guinea, intestinal parasitism. The responses given by the sample respondents have been summarized zone wise and presented accordingly in the following table:

Table 4.30: Zone wise Signs & Symptoms and Diseases

Zone	*Frequency*	*Signs and Symptoms*	*Diseases*	*Total*
Hasthampatti	No.	70	18	88
	%	79.50%	20.50%	100.00%
Ammapet	No.	45	59	104
	%	43.30%	56.70%	100.00%
Kondalampatti	No.	65	17	82
	%	79.30%	20.70%	100.00%
Suramangalam	No.	90	21	111
	%	81.10%	18.90%	100.00%
Total		**270**	**115**	**385**

Source: Compiled with Primary Data

Of the sample households, majority (70.13 percent) were largely affected by signs and symptoms and the remaining (29.87 percent) were largely affected by diseases. Among the category of households largely affected by signs and symptoms, 33.33 percent were found in Suramangalam Zone. A Majority of households in Ammapet Zone, were found to be affected by diseases largely.

It could be understood from the Table 4.30 that 79.5 percent of the households in Hasthampatti zone have been affected by signs and symptoms and 20.5 percent of them have been affected by diseases. Among the households of Ammapet zone, it has been reported that 43.3 percent of them have been suffering from signs and symptoms and 56.7 percent of them have been affected by diseases. Out of 82 households of Kondalampatti zone, there were signs and symptoms for 79.3 percent of the households and the proportion of households affected by diseases was found to be 20.7 per cent. It is understood that 81.1 percent of households in Suramangalam zone have witnessed signs and symptoms while 18.9 percent of them have been affected by diseases.

In order to examine the significance of relationship between the signs and symptoms and diseases among the four zones the following hypotheses have been framed and tested:

Null Hypothesis H_0: There is no significant relationship between the signs and symptoms and diseases among the four zones.

Alternative Hypothesis H_1: There is a significant relationship between the signs and symptoms and diseases among the four zones.

Table 4.31: Zone and Signs & Symptoms or Diseases – Chi Square Test

Factor	*Chi square value*	*DF*	*p value*	*Result*
Zone	49.168	3	0.000	Rejected **

According to the Table 4.31 the chi square value stating the relationship between the signs and symptoms and diseases among the four zones has been found to be 49.168 and the p value was 0.000. Since the p value is less than 0.01, it falls in the rejection region. Hence, the null hypothesis is rejected and the alternative hypothesis is accepted. The hypothesis that 'there is no significant relationship between the signs and symptoms and diseases among the four zones does not hold good. It implies that the signs and symptoms and diseases varied from one zone to another.

4.9 Factors determining the Impact of Improper Management of Waste on Human Health

In order to find the factors determining the perception of households that their health ailments were due to the improper waste management in their area the following explanatory variables have been selected by using binary logit regression. Since the dependent variable viz. impact of waste management on health is categorical, binary logit regression is applied.

Table 4.32: Description of Explanatory Variables

Variable	Description	Unit of Measurement	Expected Sign
Frequency of Waste Collection	Frequency of Waste Collection at Houses	1=Daily 2 = Once in Three Days 3 = Once in a Week 4 = Once in a Month	-
Perception about the Waste Management	Perception about the Waste Management of the Corporation in their Area	1 = Good 2 = Bad	-
Personal Attitude	Attitude towards Segregation and Reuse of Solid Waste	1 = Yes 2 = No	-
Quantity of Waste Generation	Quantity of Waste Generated by Households per day	1 = <500 2 = 501-1000 3 = 1001 – 1500 4 = >1501	+

The health ailments of household members due to improper management of solid waste in their locality were found to be determined by the factor viz. frequency of waste collection and disposal in their area. Greater the frequency of waste collection less will be the chance to get affected by ailments due to dumping of wastes. Thus the present study has assigned negative sign between frequency of waste collection and occurrence of diseases.

The perception of the households regarding the efficiency of waste management in their area is another important factor determining the impact of improper waste management on health conditions of household members. If the waste management is good the impact of improper waste management on health will be negative and vice versa. Thus negative sign was assumed between the efficiency of waste management and its impact on health.

If the household members attempted to segregate and reuse their waste, then the problem of waste disposal and management will be minimal. Thus its impact on health conditions of household members will be less. Thus the present study has assigned negative sign between attitude towards segregation and reuse of waste and health ailments due to improper of management of waste in their area.

The higher the quantity of waste generated by households more will be the accumulation of waste in their area, which tends to cause the improper management of waste in their area. Thus its impact on health conditions of household members will be high. The present study has assumed positive relationship between quantity of waste generated and the impact of improper of waste management on health.

Table 4.33: Description of Dependent Variable

Impact of Improper Solid Waste Management on Health	*Frequency*	*Percentage*
Yes	220	57.1
No	165	42.9
Total	**385**	**100**

Source: Compiled with Primary Data

Of the 385 sample households, 220 revealed that their health ailments were due to the improper management of waste in their area.

Table 4.34: Omnibus Tests of Model Coefficients

	Chi-square	*DF*	*Sig.*
Step	218.317	4	.000
Block	218.317	4	.000
Model	218.317	4	.000

The significant chi square value of the omnibus test suggests that the model has no explanatory power.

Table 4.35: Model Summary

Step	*-2 Log likelihood*	*Cox & Snell R Square*	*Nagelkerke R Square*
1	37.522[a]	.533	.681

The value of -2 log likelihood statistics suggests that the model is better, since its value is less.

Table 4.36: Hosmer and Lemeshow Test

Step	*Chi-square*	*DF*	*Sig.*
1	11.790	7	.108

The insignificant p value of Hosmer and Lemeshow test suggests that the data fit the model well.

Table 4.37: Variables in the Equation

Variables	*B*	*S.E.*	*Wald*	*DF*	*Sig.*	*Exp(B)*
Quantity of Waste Generated	1.542	.303	25.840	1	.012	4.674
Segregation and Reuse of Waste	-.070	.344	.041	1	.839	.932
Frequency of Waste Disposal	-1.337	.310	18.647	1	.003	.263
Perception about Waste Management	-3.026	.353	73.394	1	.023	.049
Constant	3.797	.999	14.449	1	.000	44.551

The factors viz. quantity of waste generated, frequency of waste collection and disposal and perception about the waste management of the Corporation in their area were found significant in determining the impact of improper solid waste management on health ailments. The attitude of household head towards segregation and reuse of solid waste is insignificant in determining the impact of improper solid waste management on health of household members. The quantity of waste was found positively related with the impact of improper management of waste on the health of the household members. The other factors viz. frequency of waste disposal and perception about waste management were negatively related with the dependent variable.

Table 4.38: Description of Explanatory Variables

Variable	Description	Unit of Measurement	Expected Sign
Age	Age of the Household Head	Age in years	-
Gender	Gender of the Household Head	1 = Male 2 = Female	-
Income	Total Average Monthly Income of the Household	1 = < 5000 2 = 5001 – 10000 3 = 10001 – 15000 4 = 15001 – 20000 5 = >20001	+
Education	Level of Education attained by the Household Head	1 = Illiterate 2 = School Level 3 = Graduction 4 = Post Graduation and above	+
Family Size	Total Number of Members Currently Residing in the House	Number of Individuals	+
Ownership of House	Details of the housing as Own House or Rented One	1 = Own House 2 = Rented House	-
Personal Attitude	Attitude towards Segregation and Reuse of Solid Waste	1 = Yes 2 = No	+
Quantity of Waste	Quantity of Waste Generated by Household per day	1 = <250 2 = 251 – 500 3 = 501- 750 4 = 751 -1000 5 = >1000	+

4.10 Factors Determining the Willingness to Pay for better Solid Waste Management

In order to find the factors determining willingness to pay of households the following explanatory variables have been selected by using binary logit regression. Since the dependent variable viz. willingness to pay is categorical the binary logit regression is applied.

Table 4.39: Dependent Variable

Willingness to Pay	*Frequency*	*Percentage*
Yes	177	46
No	208	54
Total	385	100

Of the 385 sample households 54 percent were unwilling to pay for better solid waste management and 46 percent were willing to pay for municipal solid waste management.

The age of the household head is expected to have a negative influence on households' willingness to pay for improved municipal solid waste management. Older generations were found more hesitant to pay for solid waste management than younger ones. The younger generations due to their better level of awareness and education about environment were willing to pay for solid waste management. Previous studies have also found that age factor had negatively influence the willingness to pay (Muhdin Muhammedhussen Batu et.al., 2016, Ojok et.al., in 2013, Ezekiel N. Nadunda and Virginia K. Muian, 2018 and Qingbin song, Zhishi Wang and Jinhui Li 2016).

Gender of the household plays a significant role in determining the willingness to pay for their family. The present study expects that the female gender will be more willing to pay for solid waste management than male. Female have more awareness and they are closer to the environment than male. Moreover women are more responsible and involved in the matter of waste disposal and management than male gender. Thus women are expected to be more willing to pay for solid waste services. The studies carried out by Qingbin Song, Zhishi Wang and Jinhui Li 2016 and Pham Thi Thuy Trang, et.al., 2017 have also found the similar nature of relationship.

Education plays a significant role in influencing the willingness to pay for solid waste management. The present study has expected the factor education to positively influence the willingness to pay for solid waste management. The higher the level of education more will be the awareness about the environment. The educated people have better understanding regarding the ill effects of improper solid waste management. Thus based on past studies, the present study has also expected that education had a positive impact on the willingness to pay (Pham Thi Thuy Trang, 2017).

Larger the size of family more will be the quantum of waste disposed. Thus it is expected that family size positively influence the willingness to pay. The past study done by Ezekiel N. Nadunda and Virginia K.Muia in 2018 has also found that family size had a significant positive impact on environment. In the studies done by Igwe Kelechi Chima, Mgbasonwu Vincent Nwabinye in 2017 and Ojok et.al., in 2013, a negative association was found between size of family and willingness to pay.

The ownership of house is also the significant factor assumed to positively influence the willingness to pay for better solid waste management. House owners have more concern about their surroundings and environment than rented households. The previous studies have also found the positive relationship between ownership of house and willingness to pay (Igwe Kelechi Chima, Mgbasonwu Vincent Nwabinye, 2017 and Muhdin Muhammedhussen Batu et.al., 2016).

The attitude of the household head regarding waste segregation and reuse is the major factor in determining the willingness to pay for solid waste management. Those who have the attitude of segregating the waste at source and reuse of waste were found to be more cautious and aware of protecting the environment. Thus the present study expected a positive relationship between attitude towards waste disposal and willingness to pay, as found by many other past studies (Bijan Maskey and Mrinila Singh, 2017 and Muhdin Muhammedhussen Batu et.al., 2016).

Table 4.40: Omnibus Tests of Model Coefficients

	Chi-square	*DF*	*Sig.*
Step	478.314	9	.000
Block	478.314	9	.000
Model	478.314	9	.000

The significant chi-square value of the above model strongly supports that the model has no explanatory power.

Table 4.41: Model Summary

Step	*-2 Log likelihood*	*Cox & Snell R Square*	*Nagelkerke R Square*
1	42.911[a]	.511	.850

The -2 loglikelihood value is 42.911. The smaller the statistic, better the model. The Cox and Snell R^2 is similar to R^2 in a multiple regression, which cannot reach the maximum of 1. But the Nagelkerke R^2 can reach the maximum of value of 1. Accordingly their value is good in the model.

Table 4.42: Hosmer and Lemeshow Test

Step	*Chi-square*	*Df*	*Sig.*
1	2.592	8	.757

The Hosmer and Lemeshow test reveals the model, well fitted with the data. The insignificant p value suggests that the data fit the model well.

Table 4.43: Variables in the Equation

Variables	*B*	*S.E.*	*Wald*	*DF*	*Sig.*	*Exp(B)*
Age	1.225	.388	9.976	1	.002	3.405
Gender	-4.414	1.729	6.516	1	.011	.012
Perception Towards Solid Waste Management	3.913	.858	20.803	1	.000	50.060
Quantity of Waste Generated	-.255	1.048	.059	1	.808	.775
Monthly House-hold Income	-2.890	.779	13.763	1	.000	.056
Personal Attitude towards Segregation of Waste	1.184	.949	1.555	1	.212	3.266
Size of Family	-.216	.315	.468	1	.494	.806
Ownership of House	5.157	.930	30.716	1	.000	173.597
Educational Qualification	-.237	.476	.247	1	.619	.789
Constant	-3.926	2.832	1.922	1	.166	.020

Dependent Variable: Willingness to Pay

Of the nine explanatory variables five variables viz. age, gender, perception towards environment, family income and ownership of house were found to be significant in determining the willingness to pay for the solid waste management. Among these factors age, perception towards waste management and ownership of house were found positively related to the willingness to pay. Gender and family income was found negatively related with the willingness to pay. The other factors viz. quantity of waste generation, attitude towards segregation and separation of solid waste, size of family and educational qualification were insignificant in determining the willingness to pay.

Table 4.44: Zone wise Willingness to Pay Extra Cost for Disposal of Solid Waste

Zone	Frequency	Less than Rs. 30	Rs. 30 to Rs. 60	Rs. 60 to Rs. 90	Above Rs. 90	Total
Hasthampatti	No.	15	3	21	1	40
	%	37.5%	7.5%	52.5%	2.5%	100.00%
Ammapet	No.	25	4	18	1	48
	%	52.08%	8.33%	37.50%	2.09%	100.00%
Kondalampatti	No.	15	4	18	1	38
	%	39.47%	10.53%	47.36%	2.64%	100.00%
Suramangalam	No.	22	6	19	4	51
	%	43.14%	11.76%	37.25%	7.85%	100.00%
Total		**77**	**17**	**76**	**7**	**177**

Source: Compiled with Primary Data

It could be understood from the Table 4.44 that out of 40 households of Hasthampatti zone, 37.5 percent of them are willing to pay less than Rs.30 per month as an extra cost for disposal of solid waste while 7.5 percent have stated that they are willing to pay Rs.30 to Rs.60 as an extra cost for disposal of solid waste and the proportion of these respondents willing to pay an extra cost of Rs.60 to Rs.90 for disposal of solid waste is found to be 52.5 per cent. It is observed that 2.5 percent of households are willing to pay an extra cost of above Rs.90 per month for disposal of solid waste.

The results reveal that among 48 households of Ammapet zone, 52.08 percent of them are willing to pay less than Rs.30 per month as an extra cost for disposal of solid waste while 8.33 percent of them have stated that they are willing to pay Rs.30 to Rs.60 as an extra cost for disposal of solid waste and the proportion of these respondents willing to pay an extra cost of Rs.60 to Rs.90 for disposal of solid waste is found to be 37.5 per cent. It is observed that 2.09 percent of these respondents are willing to pay an extra cost of above Rs.90 per month for disposal of solid waste.

It is evinced from the analysis that among 38 households of Kondalampatti zone, 39.47 percent of are willing to pay less than Rs.30 per month as an extra cost for disposal of solid waste while 10.53 percent have stated that they are willing to pay Rs.30 to Rs.60 as an extra cost for disposal of solid waste and the proportion of households willing to pay an extra cost of Rs.60 to Rs.90 for disposal of solid waste is found to be 47.36 per cent. It is observed that 2.64 percent of households are willing to pay an extra cost of above Rs.90 per month for disposal of solid waste.

The analysis indicates that out of 51 households of Suramangalam zone, 43.14 percent of them are willing to pay less than Rs.30 per month as an extra cost for disposal of solid waste while 11.76 percent of them have stated that they are willing to pay Rs.30 to Rs.60 as an extra cost for disposal of solid waste and the proportion of these households willing to pay an extra cost of Rs.60 to Rs.90 for disposal of solid waste is found to be 37.25 per cent. It is observed that 7.85 percent of these households are willing to pay an extra cost of above Rs.90 per month for disposal of solid waste.

With a view to test the significance of relationship between the willingness to pay an extra cost for disposal of solid waste among the four zones the following hypotheses have been framed and tested:

Null Hypothesis H_0: There is no significant relationship between the willingness to pay an extra cost for disposal of solid waste among the four zones.

Alternative Hypothesis H_1: There is a significant relationship between the willingness to pay an extra cost for disposal of solid waste among the four zones.

Table 4.45: Zone and Willing to pay Extra Cost for Disposal of Solid Waste – Chi Square Test

Factor	*Chi square value*	*DF*	*p value*	*Result*
Zone	9.867	9	0.361	Accepted

From the Table 4.45, it is divulged that the chi square value stating the relationship between zones and willing to pay an extra cost for disposal of solid waste has been found to be 9.867 and the p value was 0.361. Since the p value is greater than 0.05, it falls in the acceptance region. Hence, the null hypothesis is accepted. The hypothesis that 'there is no significant relationship between the willing to pay an extra cost for disposal of solid waste among the four zones holds good. It implies that the willingness to pay for an extra cost for disposal of solid waste did not vary significantly according to the zones. Households in all zones are equally willing to pay for an improved solid waste management.

Table 4.46: Monthly Income and Amount of Willingness to pay Extra Cost for Disposal of Solid Waste

Monthly Income	*Frequency*	*Less than Rs. 30*	*Rs. 30 to Rs. 60*	*Rs. 60 to Rs. 90*	*Above Rs. 90*	*Total*
Less than	No.	25	8	31	3	67
Rs. 5000	%	37.31%	11.95%	46.27%	4.47%	100.00%
Rs. 5001 to	No.	23	4	29	0	56
Rs. 10000	%	41.08%	7.14%	51.78%	0.00%	100.00%
Rs. 10001 to	No.	16	3	12	2	33
Rs. 15000	%	48.48%	9.09%	36.36%	6.07%	100.00%
Rs. 15001 to	No.	8	2	5	0	15
Rs. 20000	%	53.33%	13.33%	33.34%	0.00%	100.00%

More than	No.	4	0	1	1	6
Rs. 20000	%	66.66%	0.00%	16.67%	16.67%	100.00%
Total		**76**	**17**	**78**	**6**	**177**

Source: Compiled with Primary Data

According to the Table 4.46, out of 67 households belonging to the monthly income group of 'Less than Rs.5000', 37.31 percent are willing to pay less than Rs.30 per month as an extra cost for disposal of solid waste while 11.95 percent of them have stated that they are willing to pay Rs.30 to Rs.60 as an extra cost for disposal of solid waste and the proportion of households willing to pay an extra cost of Rs.60 to Rs.90 for disposal of solid waste is found to be 46.27 per cent. It is observed that 4.47 percent of these households are willing to pay an extra cost of above Rs.90 per month for disposal of solid waste.

The results reveal that among 56 households pertaining to the monthly income group of 'Rs.5001 to Rs.10000', 41.08 percent are willing to pay less than Rs.30 per month as an extra cost for disposal of solid waste while 7.14 percent of them have stated that they are willing to pay Rs.30 to Rs.60 as an extra cost for disposal of solid waste and the proportion of households willing to pay an extra cost of Rs.60 to Rs.90 for disposal of solid waste is found to be 51.78 per cent. It is observed that none of the households are willing to pay an extra cost of above Rs.90 per month for disposal of solid waste.

It is evinced from the analysis that among 33 households earning a monthly income of 'Rs.10001 to Rs.15000', 48.48 percent of them are willing to pay less than Rs.30 per month as an extra cost for disposal of solid waste while 9.09 percent of them have stated that they are willing to pay Rs.30 to Rs.60 as an extra cost for disposal of solid waste and the proportion of the households willing to pay an extra cost of Rs.60 to Rs.90 for disposal of solid waste is found to be 36.36 per cent. It is observed that

6.07 percent of the households are willing to pay an extra cost of above Rs.90 per month for disposal of solid waste.

The analysis indicates that out of 15 households belonging to the monthly income group of 'Rs.15001 to Rs.20000' 53.33 percent are willing to pay less than Rs.30 per month as an extra cost for disposal of solid waste while 13.33 percent have stated that they are willing to pay Rs.30 to Rs.60 as an extra cost for disposal of solid waste and the proportion of households willing to pay an extra cost of Rs.60 to Rs.90 for disposal of solid waste is found to be 33.34 per cent. It is observed that none of the households are willing to pay an extra cost of above Rs.90 per month for disposal of solid waste.

The results reveal that among six households pertaining to the monthly income group of 'More than Rs.20000', 66.66 percent of them are willing to pay less than Rs.30 per month as an extra cost for disposal of solid waste while none of them have stated that they are willing to pay Rs.30 to Rs.60 as an extra cost for disposal of solid waste and the proportion of the households willingness to pay an extra cost of Rs.60 to Rs.90 for disposal of solid waste is found to be 16.67 per cent. It is observed that 16.67 percent of the households are willing to pay an extra cost of above Rs.90 per month for disposal of solid waste.

With a view to test the significance of relationship between monthly income and willingness to pay an extra cost for disposal of solid waste the following hypotheses have been framed and tested:

Null Hypothesis H_0: There is no significant relationship between monthly income of households and amount of willingness to pay for disposal of solid waste.

Alternative Hypothesis H_1: There is a significant relationship between monthly income of households and the amount of willingness to pay for disposal of solid waste.

Table 4.47: Monthly Income and Amount of Willingness to Pay for Disposal of Solid Waste – Chi Square Test

Factor	*Chi square value*	*DF*	*p value*	*Result*
Monthly Income	24.91	12	0.015	Rejected *

Table 4.47 proclaims that the chi square value stating the relationship between monthly income of households and the amount of willingness to pay for disposal of solid waste has been found to be 24.91 and the p value was 0.015. Since the p value is less than 0.05, it falls in the rejection region. Hence, the null hypothesis is rejected and the alternative hypothesis is accepted. The hypothesis that 'there is no significant relationship between monthly income and amount of willingness to pay for disposal of solid waste' does not hold good. It denotes that the amount of willingness to pay for disposal of solid waste varied significantly according to the monthly income.

Table 4.48: Educational Level and Amount of Willingness to Pay for Disposal of Solid Waste

Educational Level	*Frequency*	*Less than Rs. 30*	*Rs. 30 to Rs. 60*	*Rs. 60 to Rs. 90*	*Above Rs. 90*	*Total*
Illiterates	No.	27	7	34	3	71
	%	38.03%	9.86%	47.88%	4.23%	100.00%
School Level	No.	9	2	17	1	29
	%	31.03%	6.89%	58.63%	3.45%	100.00%
Graduation	No.	17	2	14	1	34
	%	50%	5.88%	41.17%	2.95%	100.00%
Post graduation	No.	24	6	12	1	43
and above	%	55.82%	13.96%	27.90%	2.32%	100.00%
Total		**77**	**17**	**77**	**6**	**177**

Source: Compiled with Primary Data

It could be realized from the Table 4.48, out of 71 illiterate household heads 38.03 percent are willing to pay less than Rs.30 per month as an extra cost for disposal of solid waste while 9.86 percent have stated that they are willing to pay Rs.30 to Rs.60 as an extra cost for disposal of solid waste and the proportion of households willing to pay an extra cost of Rs.60 to Rs.90 for disposal of solid waste is found to be 47.88 per cent. It is observed that 4.23 percent of respondents are willing to pay an extra cost of above Rs.90 per month for disposal of solid waste.

The results reveal that among 29 household heads who had school level education 31.03 percent of them are willing to pay less than Rs.30 per month as an extra cost for disposal of solid waste while 6.89 percent have stated that they are willing to pay Rs.30 to Rs.60 as an extra cost for disposal of solid waste and the proportion of these respondents willing to pay an extra cost of Rs.60 to Rs.90 for disposal of solid waste is found to be 58.63 per cent. It is observed that 3.45 percent of respondents are willing to pay an extra cost of above Rs.90 per month for disposal of solid waste.

It is evinced from the analysis that among 34 household heads who have been graduated 50 percent of them are willing to pay less than Rs.30 per month as an extra cost for disposal of solid waste while 5.88 percent of them have stated that they are willing to pay Rs.30 to Rs.60 as an extra cost for disposal of solid waste and the proportion of the households willing to pay an extra cost of Rs.60 to Rs.90 for disposal of solid waste is found to be 41.17 per cent. It is observed that 2.95 percent of households are willing to pay an extra cost of above Rs.90 per month for disposal of solid waste.

The analysis indicates that out of 43 respondents who have been qualified for the post graduation and above, 55.82 percent of them are willing to pay less than Rs.30 per month as an extra cost for disposal of solid waste while 13.96 percent of them have stated that they are willing to pay Rs.30 to Rs.60 as an extra cost for disposal of solid waste and the proportion of households willing to pay an extra cost of Rs.60 to Rs.90 for disposal of solid waste is found to be 27.90 per cent. It is observed that 2.32 percent of households are willing to pay an extra cost of above Rs.90 per month for disposal of solid waste.

With a view to test the significance of relationship between educational level and amount of willingness to pay for disposal of solid waste the following hypotheses have been framed and tested:

Null Hypothesis H_0: There is no significant relationship between educational level and amount of willingness to pay for disposal of solid waste.

Alternative Hypothesis H_1: There is a significant relationship between educational level and amount of willingness to pay for disposal of solid waste.

Table 4.49: Educational Level and Amount of Willingness to Pay for Disposal of Solid Waste – Chi Square Test

Factor	*Chi square value*	*DF*	*p value*	*Result*
Educational Level	20.715	9	0.014	Rejected *

According to the Table 4.49 the chi square value stating the relationship between educational levels and amount of willingness to pay an extra cost for disposal of solid waste has been found to be 20.715 and the p value was 0.014. Since the p value is less than 0.05, it falls in the rejection region. Hence, the null hypothesis is rejected and the alternative hypothesis is accepted. The hypothesis that 'there is no significant relationship between educational level and amount of willingness to pay for disposal of solid waste' does not hold good. It denotes that the amount of willingness to pay for disposal of solid waste varied significantly according to the different levels of education.

Table 4.50: Occupational Status and Amount of Willingness to Pay for Disposal of Solid Waste

Occupational Level	*Frequency*	*Less than Rs. 30*	*Rs. 30 to Rs. 60*	*Rs. 60 to Rs. 90*	*Above Rs. 90*	*Total*
Coolies	No.	29	8	39	3	79
	%	36.71%	10.13%	49.37%	3.79%	100.00%
Farmers	No.	7	1	13	1	22
	%	31.81%	4.55%	59.09%	4.55%	100.00%
Business	No.	14	3	5	1	23
	%	60.86%	13.05%	21.74%	4.35%	100.00%
Employees	No.	17	4	16	0	37
	%	45.94%	10.82%	43.24%	0.00%	100.00%
Profession	No.	10	1	4	1	16
	%	62.5%	6.25%	25%	6.25%	100.00%
Total		77	17	77	6	177

Source: Compiled with Primary Data.

Table 4.50 divulges that out of 79 household heads occupied as coolies 36.71 percent are willing to pay less than Rs.30 per month as an extra cost for disposal of solid waste while 10.13 percent of them have stated that they are willing to pay Rs.30 to Rs.60 as an extra cost for disposal of solid waste and the proportion of the households willing to pay an extra cost of Rs.60 to Rs.90 for disposal of solid waste is found to be 49.37 per cent. It is observed that 3.79 percent of these respondents are willing to pay an extra cost of above Rs.90 per month for disposal of solid waste.

The results reveal that among 22 household heads who were farmers 31.81 percent are willing to pay less than Rs.30 per month as extra an cost for disposal of solid waste while 4.55 percent of them have stated that they are willing to pay Rs.30 to Rs.60 as an extra cost for disposal of solid waste and the proportion of these respondents willing to pay an extra cost of Rs.60 to Rs.90 for disposal of solid waste is found to be 59.09 per cent.

It is observed that 4.55 percent of these respondents are willing to pay an extra cost of above Rs.90 per month for disposal of solid waste.

It is evinced from the analysis that among 23 household heads engaged in business 60.86 percent are willing to pay less than Rs.30 per month as an extra cost for disposal of solid waste while 13.05 percent have stated that they are willing to pay Rs.30 to Rs.60 as an extra cost for disposal of solid waste and the proportion of households willing to pay an extra cost of Rs.60 to Rs.90 for disposal of solid waste is found to be 21.74 per cent. It is observed that 4.35 percent of households are willing to pay an extra cost of above Rs.90 per month for disposal of solid waste.

The analysis indicates that out of 37 household heads in the category of employees 45.94 percent are willing to pay less than Rs.30 per month as an extra cost for disposal of solid waste while 10.82 percent of them have stated that they are willing to pay Rs.30 to Rs.60 as an extra cost for disposal of solid waste and the proportion of the households respondents willing to pay an extra cost of Rs.60 to Rs.90 for disposal of solid waste is found to be 43.24 per cent. It is observed that none of the households are willing to pay an extra cost of above Rs.90 per month for disposal of solid waste.

The results reveal that among 16 respondents occupied as professionals 62.5 percent of them are willing to pay less than Rs.30 per month as an extra cost for disposal of solid waste while 6.25 percent of them have stated that they are willing to pay Rs.30 to Rs.60 as an extra cost for disposal of solid waste and the proportion of the households willing to pay an extra cost of Rs.60 to Rs.90 for disposal of solid waste is found to be 25 per cent. It is observed that 6.25 percent of the households are willing to pay an extra cost of above Rs.90 per month for disposal of solid waste.

With a view to test the significance of relationship between the occupational status of the household heads and amount of willingness to pay for disposal of solid waste the following hypotheses have been framed and tested:

Null Hypothesis H_0: There is no significant relationship between occupational status and the amount of willingness to pay for disposal of solid waste.

Alternative Hypothesis H_1: There is a significant relationship between occupational status and amount of willingness to pay for disposal of solid waste.

Table 4.51: Occupational Status and Amount of Willingness to Pay for Disposal of Solid Waste – Chi Square Test

Factor	*Chi square value*	*DF*	*p value*	*Result*
Occupational Status	25.12	12	0.014	Rejected *

It is implied from the Table 4.51 that the chi square value stating the relationship between occupational status and amount of willingness to pay for disposal of solid waste has been found to be 25.12 and the p value was 0.014. Since the p value is less than 0.05, it falls in the rejection region. Hence, the null hypothesis is rejected and the alternative hypothesis is accepted. The hypothesis that 'there is no significant relationship between occupational status and amount of willingness to pay for disposal of solid waste' does not hold good. It denotes that the amount of willingness to pay for disposal of solid waste varied significantly according to the occupational statuses of the household heads.

Table 4.52: Zone wise Reasons for Willingness to Pay Extra Cost

Zone	*Frequency*	*Inadequacy of Current Municipal Solid Management*	*For better Environmental Management*	*To improve Health Condition, Affected by Improper Solid Wmaste Management*	*Total*
Hasthampatti	No.	10	14	16	40
	%	25%	35%	40%	100.00%
Ammapet	No.	13	17	18	48
	%	27.08%	35.42%	37.5%	100.00%
Kondalampatti	No.	11	14	13	38
	%	28.94%	36.84%	34.22%	100.00%
Suramangalam	No.	14	20	17	51
	%	27.45%	39.21%	33.34%	100.00%
Total		**48**	**65**	**64**	**177**

Source: Compiled with Primary Data.

The major reasons attributed for the willingness to pay an extra cost for solid waste management were improvement in health conditions and better environmental management.

H_0 = There is no significant relationship between the reasons attributed for the willingness to pay among the households in different zones.

H1 = There is a significant relationship between the reasons attributed for the willingness to pay among the households in different zones.

Table 4.53: Zone and Reasons for Willing to Pay Extra Cost – Chi Square Test

Factor	*Chi square value*	*DF*	*p value*	*Result*
Zone	2.002	6	0.919	Accepted

Since the p value is greater than 0.05, it falls in the acceptance region. Thus the null hypothesis is accepted.

It was found that there is no significant difference in the reasons attributed for the willingness to pay for solid waste management among the four zones.

From the analysis of primary data collected from the households in Salem Corporation, it was found that there was a significant difference in the quantum of solid waste generated by households among the four zones. Households' perception regarding the performance of solid waste was found to be significantly different among four zones. The major determinants of solid waste generation by households were family income, size of family, educational qualification and personal attitudes towards sorting and recycling of solid waste. The impact of improper solid waste management on health ailments is determined by the factors viz. quantity of waste generation, frequency of waste collection and disposal and perception about the waste management of the Corporation in their area. The factors determining the willingness to pay for better management of solid waste by households were age, gender, perception towards environment, family income and ownership of house.

5

Analyis of Health Concerns of Sanitary Workers

Sanitary workers are the workers employed by the Municipal Corporation for performing sanitary works in the municipal limits. Salem Municipal Corporation has employed the sanitary workers mainly for sweeping, collecting and loading domestic garbage. Those who are employed in the sweeping work have to clean the streets up to the specified limit while the workers engaged in collection of domestic garbage need to go for door to door garbage collection. The size of streets for the sanitary workers is determined on the basis of the number of houses. The sanitary workers, who are assigned the loading work, have to load the garbage in huge dust bins.

5.1 Health Hazards of Sanitary Workers

In this chapter, the health concerns of the sanitary workers have been analyzed and interpreted. It consists of the analysis of the profile of the sanitary workers, their health conditions and provision of sanitary materials. In the first part, the relationships between the profile of the sanitary workers and their health conditions have been analyzed using chi square test. For this purpose, the profile of the sanitary workers included age, gender, educational level, monthly income and nature of work. Health conditions of the sanitary workers have been measured by obtaining the level of agreement of the respondents for the following statements:

1. I have been injured while performing the sanitary work
2. I have been suffering from temporary illness due to the sanitary work
3. I have been affected by acute illness due to the sanitary work
4. I always go to Government hospital for getting treatment for the ailment.
5. I have to start the sanitary work in the very early morning.
6. I have been given excessive workload.

The level of agreement of respondents to these statements has been obtained in a five-point scale as Strongly Agree (SA), Agree (A), Neutral (N), Disagree (DA) and Strongly Disagree (SDA). The scores assigned to these statements were 5 for Strongly Agree; 4 for Agree; 3 for Neutral; 2 for Disagree; and 1 for Strongly Disagree.

Table 5.1: Age and Injury Details of the Sanitary Workers

Age	Frequency	SA	A	N	DA	SDA	Total
Below 25 years	No.	9	11	0	2	2	24
	%	37.50%	45.90%	0.00%	8.30%	8.30%	100.00%
25 to 35 years	No.	12	22	6	6	10	56
	%	21.40%	39.30%	10.70%	10.70%	17.90%	100.00%
35 to 50 years	No.	17	40	4	10	5	76
	%	22.40%	52.60%	5.30%	13.20%	6.60%	100.00%
Above 50 years	No.	13	18	1	3	2	37
	%	35.10%	48.60%	2.70%	8.10%	5.40%	100.00%
Total		**51**	**91**	**11**	**21**	**19**	**193**

Source: Compiled with Primary Data

Around 39.37 percent of the sample sanitary workers were in the age group of 35 to 50 years, since there was no fresh appointment in recent times on permanent basis. Even though sanitary workers have been newly recruited in recent times, they were employed only under the contract basis by private firms. Thus the sanitary workers in the younger age group below 25 years were employed under contract basis. Regarding the opinion of being injured while doing sanitary work, around 47.15 percent have agreed followed by the category of strongly agreed [i.e. 26.42 per cent].

From the Table 5.1, it could be understood that out of 24 respondents in the age group of below 25 years, 37.5 percent have strongly agreed while 45.9 percent of them have agreed. Disagreement was expressed by 8.3 percent of these respondents and strong disagreement was stated by another 8.3 percent of these respondents. It reveals that in the age group of below 25 years, the major proportion of the respondents have agreed that they have got injury while performing the sanitary work.

Out of 56 respondents pertaining to the age group of 25 to 35 years, 21.4 percent of them have strongly agreed whereas 39.3 percent of them have agreed and 10.7 percent of them have neutral status. Among these respondents 10.7 percent of them have disagreed and 17.9 percent of them have strongly disagreed. It implies that major proportion of the respondents belonging to this age group have agreed that they have been injured while performing the sanitary work.

Among 76 respondents falling under the age group of 35 to 50 years, 22.4 percent of them have strongly agreed while 52.6 percent of them have agreed and neutrality has been maintained by 5.3 percent of such respondents. It is noted that 13.2 percent of these respondents have disagreed and 6.6 percent of them have strongly disagreed. It implies that majority of the respondents in this group have agreed that they have been injured while performing the sanitary work.

It is observed that out of 37 respondents belonging to the age group of 'Above 50 years', 35.1 percent of them have strongly agreed whereas 48.6 percent of them have agreed and 2.7 percent of the respondents did not express neither agreement nor disagreement. Further, there were 8.1 percent of respondents who have disagreed and 5.4 percent of them have strongly disagreed. It denotes that the major proportion of these respondents agreed that they have been injured while performing the sanitary work.

With a view to understand the significance of relationship between the age of the respondents and their level of agreement to the injury while performing the sanitary work, the following hypotheses have been framed and tested:

Null Hypothesis H_0: There is no significant relationship between the age of the respondents and their level of agreement to injury while performing the sanitary work.

Alternative Hypothesis H_1: There is a significant relationship between the age of the respondents and their level of agreement to injury while performing the sanitary work.

Table 5.2: Relationship between Age and Injury while Performing the Sanitary Work – Chi Square Test

Factor	*Chi square value*	*DF*	*P value*	*Result*
Age	14.911	12	0.246	Accepted

Table 5.2 evinces that the computed value of chi square was 14.911 and the p value indicating the relationship between the age of the respondents and the agreement to injury while performing the sanitary work was found to be 0.246. Since the p value is greater than 0.05, it falls in the acceptance region. Hence, the null hypothesis is accepted and it is concluded that there exists no significant relationship between the age of the sanitary workers and the injury while performing the sanitary work. It indicates

that getting injured while performing the sanitary work is common to all the age groups of the sanitary workers.

Table 5.3: Relationship between Gender and Injury while Performing the Sanitary Work

Gender	*Frequency*	*SA*	*A*	*N*	*DA*	*SDA*	*Total*
Male	No.	22	35	7	10	11	85
	%	25.90%	41.20%	8.20%	11.80%	12.90%	100.00%
Female	No.	29	56	4	11	8	108
	%	26.90%	51.90%	3.70%	10.20%	7.40%	100.00%
Total		**51**	**91**	**11**	**21**	**19**	**193**

Source: Compiled with Primary Data

Of the total sample workers, around 56 percent were women. Women sanitary workers were allotted sanitary works like street sweeping and door to door collection of wastes and men were allotted works like public toilet cleaning, sewage cleaning and disposing wastes at the dumping yards. Since the major portion of waste management activities in the Corporation include collection of garbage from households, majority sample workers were found to be women.

Table 5.3 evinces that out of 85 male respondents, 25.9 percent of them have strongly agreed that they were injured while performing the sanitary work and 41.2 percent of such respondents have agreed while 8.2 percent of them have neither agreed nor disagreed. Out of these respondents 11.80 percent of them have disagreed and 12.90 percent of them have strongly disagreed that they have got injury while performing the sanitary work.

Among 108 female workers, 26.9 percent of them have strongly agreed that they were injured while performing the sanitary work whereas 51.9 percent of them have agreed and 3.7 percent of them maintained neutrality. About 10.20 percent of them have disagreed that they were injured while performing the sanitary work and 7.4 percent of them have strongly disagreed.

In order to understand the significance of relationship between the gender of the sanitary workers and the level of agreement to injury while performing the sanitary work, the following hypotheses have been framed and tested:

Null Hypothesis H_0: There is no significant relationship between the gender of the sanitary workers and their level of agreement to injury while performing the sanitary work.

Alternative Hypothesis H_1: There is a significant relationship between the gender of the sanitary workers and their level of agreement to injury while performing the sanitary work.

Table 5.4: Relationship between Gender and Injury while Performing the Sanitary Work – Chi Square Test

Factor	*Chi square*	*DF*	*p value*	*Result*
Gender	4.469	4	0.346	Accepted

From the Table 5.4, it is observed that the p value stating the relationship between the gender and level of agreement to injury while performing the sanitary work was 0.346. Since the p value is greater than 0.05, it falls in the acceptance region. Hence, the null hypothesis is accepted and it is concluded that there exists no significant relationship between the gender of the sanitary workers and their level of agreement to injury while performing the sanitary work. Thus it can be interpreted that their injury was not determined by their gender.

Table 5.5: Relationship between 'Educational Level and Injury while Performing the Sanitary Work

Educational Level	*Frequency*	*SA*	*A*	*N*	*DA*	*SDA*	*Total*
No formal education	No.	30	37	4	8	10	89
	%	33.70%	41.60%	4.50%	9.00%	11.20%	100.00%
Elementary Level	No.	14	42	4	7	6	73
	%	19.20%	57.50%	5.50%	9.60%	8.20%	100.00%

High School Level	No.	6	10	2	5	3	26
	%	23.10%	38.50%	7.70%	19.20%	11.50%	100.00%
Hr. Sec. Level	No.	1	2	1	1	0	5
	%	20.00%	40.00%	20.00%	20.00%	0.00%	100.00%
Total		**51**	**91**	**11**	**21**	**19**	**193**

Source: Compiled with Primary Data

Around 46.11 percent of sanitary workers failed to receive any formal education. Of this category a few were capable of putting their signature though they haven't received formal education. Around 38 percent have had their elementary level of education.

It is divulged from the Table 5.5 that out of 89 sanitary workers having no formal education, 33.7 percent of them have strongly agreed to the injury while performing the sanitary work whereas 41.6 percent of them have agreed and 4.5 percent of these workers have neither expressed agreement nor disagreement. On the other hand, disagreement was felt by 9 percent of these workers and strong disagreement was found among 11.2 percent of such workers.

Among 73 sanitary workers who had their education at the elementary level, 19.2 percent of them have strong agreement about the injury while performing the sanitary work whereas 57.5 percent of these workers have agreed and 5.5 percent of them have kept neutrality. About 9.6 percent of them have disagreed and 8.2 percent of these workers have strongly disagreed that they were injured while performing the sanitary work.

In the case of 26 sanitary workers who have completed high school level of education, 23.1 percent of them have strongly agreed and 38.5 percent of them have agreed while 7.7 percent of them were neutral. The proportion of these workers who have disagreed that they were injured while performing the sanitary work was found to be 19.2 percent and that of strongly disagreed sanitary workers was 11.5 per cent.

There were only 5 sanitary workers who have completed higher secondary level education. Among them, 20 percent have strongly agreed that injury was caused to them while performing the sanitary work whereas 40 percent have agreed to this statement and 20 percent have neither agreed nor disagreed.

With a view to ensure the above observation, the following hypotheses have been framed and tested:

Null Hypothesis H_0: There is no significant relationship between the educational level and the agreement to injury while performing the sanitary work.

Alternative Hypothesis H_1: There is a significant relationship between the educational level and the agreement to injury while performing the sanitary work.

Table 5.6: Relationship between Educational Level and Injury while Performing the Sanitary Work – Chi Square Test

Factor	*Chi square*	*DF*	*p value*	*Result*
Educational Level	11.753	12	0.466	Accepted

According to the Table 5.6, the computed value of chi square and p value indicating the relationship between the educational level and the injury while performing the sanitary work were 11.753 and 0.466 respectively. The null hypothesis is accepted as the p value is found to be greater than 0.05. The hypothesis that 'the educational level and the injury while performing sanitary work are not significantly related' holds good. Hence, it is concluded that injury while performing the sanitary work is not greater to any specific group of sanitary workers categorized by educational level.

Table 5.7: Relationship between Monthly income and Injury while Performing the Sanitary Work

Monthly Income	*Frequency*	*SA*	*A*	*N*	*DA*	*SDA*	*Total*
Below Rs. 6000	No.	5	7	1	1	0	14
	%	35.70%	50.00%	7.10%	7.10%	0.00%	100.00%

Rs.6000 to Rs. 12000	No.	11	13	1	2	2	29
	%	37.90%	44.80%	3.40%	6.90%	6.90%	100.00%
Rs.12000 to Rs. 18000	No.	20	42	7	11	12	92
	%	21.70%	45.70%	7.60%	12.00%	13.00%	100.00%
Above Rs. 18000	No.	15	29	2	7	5	58
	%	25.90%	50.00%	3.40%	12.10%	8.60%	100.00%
Total		51	91	11	21	19	193

Source: Compiled with Primary Data

Around 47.66 percent of the sanitary workers have received their monthly income in the range of Rs. 12000 to 18000. The workers 14 in numbers out of 193, who were receiving monthly income less than Rs. 6000 were contract workers employed by private firms. The sanitary workers employed by corporation are receiving more income on the basis of their experience ranging from Rs. 10000 to 35000. The difference in the pay of the corporation workers was not due to the nature of works they are assigned. The contract workers were given daily wages on the basis of the work they were assigned.

Table 5.7 depicts that out of 14 sanitary workers earning a monthly income of below Rs.6000, 35.7 percent have strongly agreed that they were injured while performing the sanitary work whereas 50 percent have agreed and 7.1 percent households have neither agreed nor disagreed. The proportion of these workers who have disagreed that they were injured while performing the sanitary work was found to be 7.1 per cent.

Among 29 sanitary workers categorized by monthly income as 'Rs.6000 to Rs.12000', the strong disagreement to the injury while performing the sanitary work was found among 37.9 percent and agreement was expressed by 44.8 percent of these workers whereas neutral response was given by 3.4 percent of such workers. About 6.9 percent of workers have disagreed and another 6.9 percent have strongly disagreed that they were injured while performing the sanitary work.

It could be understood that out of 92 sanitary workers categorized under 'Rs.12000 to Rs.18000' monthly income group, 21.7 percent have strongly agreed that they were injured while performing sanitary work whereas 45.7 percent agreed and 7.6 percent of expressed neutral opinion. About 12 percent have disagreed and 13 percent have strongly disagreed that they were injured while performing the sanitary work.

The results show that out of 58 sanitary workers pertaining to the monthly income group of 'Above Rs.18000', 25.9 percent of them have strongly agreed and 50 percent of them have agreed while 3.40 percent of respondents kept neutrality. Around 12.1 percent of workers have disagreed and 8.6 percent of such workers have strongly disagreed that injury was caused to them while performing the sanitary work.

With a view to examine the relationship between the monthly income and injury while performing the sanitary work, the following hypotheses have been framed and tested:

Null Hypothesis H_0: There is no significant relationship between the monthly income and agreement to injury while performing the sanitary work.

Alternative Hypothesis H_1: There is a significant relationship between the monthly income and agreement to injury while performing the sanitary work.

Table 5.8: Relationship between Monthly Income and Injury while Performing the Sanitary Work – Chi Square Test

Factor	*Chi square*	*DF*	*p value*	*Result*
Monthly Income	7.75	12	0.804	Accepted

It is proclaimed that the value of chi square computed to be 7.75 while the p value notifying the relationship between the monthly income and injury while performing the sanitary work was found to be 0.804. Since the p value exceeds 0.05, the null hypothesis is accepted. Thus it could be concluded that the relationship between the monthly income and injury while performing the sanitary work is not significant. It denotes that the injury while performing the sanitary work is common to all the sanitary workers grouped by their monthly income.

Table 5.9: Relationship between Nature of Work and Injury while Performing the Sanitary Work

Nature of Work	*Frequency*	*SA*	*A*	*N*	*DA*	*SDA*	*Total*
Sweeping	No.	20	19	3	5	3	50
	%	40.00%	38.00%	6.00%	10.00%	6.00%	100.00%
Collection	No.	15	42	5	10	12	84
	%	17.90%	50.00%	6.00%	11.90%	14.30%	100.00%
Loading	No.	16	30	3	6	4	59
	%	27.10%	50.80%	5.10%	10.20%	6.80%	100.00%
Total		**51**	**91**	**11**	**21**	**19**	**193**

Source: Compiled with Primary Data

It is evinced from the Table 5.9 that out of 50 sweepers, 40 percent of them have strongly agreed that they were injured while performing the sanitary work whereas 38 percent of these workers have agreed and 6 percent of such workers have responded neutrally. About 10 percent of these workers have disagreed that injury was caused while performing the sanitary work whereas 6 percent of the sweepers have strongly disagreed that performing the sanitary work has caused injury to them.

Among 84 garbage collection workers, 17.9 percent expressed strong agreement towards injury while performing the sanitary work whereas 50 percent have agreed and 6 percent have given neutral response. Around 11.9 percent have disagreed and 14.3 percent have strongly disagreed that they were injured while performing the sanitary work.

Out of 59 sanitary workers engaged in loading of the solid waste, 27.1 percent have strongly agreed and 50.8

percent have agreed that the sanitary work has caused injury to them. However, 5.1 percent of them have no opinion about the injury due to sanitary work. About 10.2 percent of these workers have disagreed and 6.8 percent of such workers have strongly disagreed that they were injured on account of performing the sanitary work.

It could be understood that the agreement was greater among the sweepers and the loading workers while disagreement was higher among the collection workers.

With a view to examine this assertion, the following hypotheses have been framed and tested:

Null Hypothesis H_0: There is no significant relationship between the nature of work and injury while performing the sanitary work

Alternative Hypothesis H_1: There is a significant relationship between the nature of work and injury while performing the sanitary work.

Table 5.10: Relationship between Nature of Work and Injury while Performing the Sanitary Work – Chi Square Test

Factor	*Chi square*	*DF*	*p value*	*Result*
Nature of Work	10.232	8	0.249	Accepted

It could be proclaimed from the Table 5.10 that the computed value of chi square was 10.232 and the p value measuring the relationship between the nature of work and injury while performing the sanitary work was ascertained to be 0.249. The p value is found to be greater than 0.05 which results in the acceptance of null hypothesis. The conclusion thus drawn from this result is that there is no significant difference in the injury caused while performing the sanitary work among the selected workers categorized by the nature of work.

Table 5.11: Relationship between Age and Suffering from Temporary Illness due to Sanitary Work

Nature of Work	*Frequency*	*SA*	*A*	*N*	*DA*	*SDA*	*Total*
Below 25 years	No.	10	9	1	2	2	24
	%	41.70%	37.50%	4.20%	8.30%	8.30%	100.00%
25 to 35 years	No.	7	20	11	6	12	56
	%	12.50%	35.70%	19.60%	10.70%	21.40%	100.00%
35 to 50 years	No.	16	36	2	9	13	76
	%	21.10%	47.40%	2.60%	11.80%	17.10%	100.00%
Above 50 years	No.	13	11	2	9	2	37
	%	35.10%	29.70%	5.40%	24.30%	5.40%	100.00%
Total		**46**	**76**	**16**	**26**	**29**	**193**

Source: Compiled with Primary Data

Regarding the statement of suffering from temporary illness due to sanitary work, around 39.37 percent have agreed followed by 23.83 percent who have strongly agreed. The sanitary workers were prone to temporary illnesses due to the nature of work they were performing. Moreover the provision of sanitary materials like boots, gloves, caps etc. will save the workers to some extent from being affected by the chronic illnesses.

From the Table 5.11, it could be understood that out of 24 respondents in the age group of below 25 years, 41.7 percent of them have strongly agreed while 37.5 percent of them have agreed and 4.2 percent of them were neutral. Disagreement was expressed by 8.3 percent of these respondents and strong disagreement was stated by another 8.3 percent of these respondents. It reveals that in the age group of below 25 years, the major proportion of the respondents have agreed that they were suffering from temporary illness due to the sanitary work.

Out of 56 respondents pertaining to the age group of 25 to 35 years, 12.5 percent of them have strongly agreed whereas 35.7 percent of them have agreed and 19.6 percent of them have neutral status. Among these respondents

10.7 percent of them have disagreed and 21.4 percent of them have strongly disagreed. It implies that major proportion of the respondents belonging to this age group have agreed that they have been suffering from temporary illness due to the sanitary work.

Among 76 respondents falling under the age group of 35 to 50 years, 21.1 percent have strongly agreed while 47.4 percent of them have agreed and neutrality has been maintained by 2.6 percent of such respondents. It is noted that 11.8 percent of respondents have disagreed and 17.1 percent of them have strongly disagreed. It implies that a majority of the respondents in this group have agreed that they have been suffering from temporary illness due to the sanitary work.

It is observed that out of 37 respondents belonging to the age group of 'Above 50 years', 35.1 percent of them have strongly agreed whereas 29.7 percent of them have agreed and 5.4 percent of the respondents did not express agreement nor disagreement. Further, there were 24.3 percent of respondents who have disagreed and 5.4 percent of them have strongly disagreed. It denotes that the major proportion of these respondents agreed that they have been suffering from temporary illness due to the sanitary work.

With a view to understand the significance of relationship between the age of the respondents and their level of agreement to the temporary illness due to the sanitary work, the following hypotheses have been framed and tested:

Null Hypothesis H_0: There is no significant relationship between the age of the respondents and suffering from temporary illness due to the sanitary work.

Alternative Hypothesis H_1: There is a significant relationship between the age of the respondents and suffering from temporary illness due to the sanitary work.

Table 5.12: Relationship between Age and Suffering from Temporary Illness due to Sanitary Work – Chi Square Test

Factor	*Chi square*	*DF*	*p value*	*Result*
Age	32.186	12	0.001	Rejected

Table 5.12 evinces that the computed value of chi square was 32.186 and the p value indicating the relationship between the age of the respondents and agreement to injury while performing the sanitary work was found to be 0.001. Since the p value is less than 0.05, it falls in the rejection region. Hence, the null hypothesis is rejected and it is concluded that there exists a significant relationship between the age of the sanitary workers and suffering from temporary illness due to the sanitary work. It indicates that the suffering from temporary illness due to the sanitary work is different among the different age groups of sanitary workers.

Table 5.13: Gender and Suffering from Temporary Illness due to Sanitary Work

Gender	*Frequency*	*SA*	*A*	*N*	*DA*	*SDA*	*Total*
Male	No.	17	37	5	15	11	85
	%	20.00%	43.50%	5.90%	17.60%	12.90%	100.00%
Female	No.	29	39	11	11	18	108
	%	26.90%	36.10%	10.20%	10.20%	16.70%	100.00%
Total		**46**	**76**	**16**	**26**	**29**	**193**

Source: Compiled with Primary Data

Table 5.13 portrays that out of 85 male respondents, 20.0 percent have strongly agreed that they were suffering from temporary illness due to the sanitary work and 43.5 percent of such respondents have agreed while 5.9 percent of them have neither agreed nor disagreed. Out of these respondents 17.6 percent of them have disagreed and 12.9

percent of them have strongly disagreed that they have got temporary illness due to the sanitary work.

Among 108 female workers, 26.9 percent have strongly agreed that they have been suffering from temporary illness due to sanitary work whereas 36.1 percent have agreed and 10.2 percent of them maintained neutrality. About 10.20 percent have disagreed that they were suffering from temporary illness due to the sanitary work and 16.7 percent have strongly disagreed.

In order to understand the significance of relationship between the age of the sanitary workers and the level of agreement to suffering from temporary illness due to the sanitary work, the following hypotheses have been framed and tested:

Null Hypothesis H_0: There is no significant relationship between the age of the sanitary workers and suffering from temporary illness due to the sanitary work.

Alternative Hypothesis H_1: There is a significant relationship between the age of the sanitary workers and suffering from temporary illness due to the sanitary work.

Table 5.14: Gender and Suffering from Temporary Illness due to Sanitary Work – Chi Square Test

Factor	*Chi square*	*DF*	*p value*	*Result*
Gender	5.069	4	0.28	Accepted

From the Table 5.14, it is observed that the p value stating the relationship between gender and level of agreement to suffering from temporary illness due to the sanitary work was 0.28. Since the p value is greater than 0.05, it falls in the acceptance region. Hence, the null hypothesis is accepted and it is concluded that there exists no significant relationship between the gender of the sanitary workers and suffering from temporary illness due to the sanitary work.

Table 5.15: Educational Level and Suffering from Temporary Illness due to Sanitary Work

Educational Level	*Frequency*	*SA*	*A*	*N*	*DA*	*SDA*	*Total*
No formal Education	No.	24	34	6	13	12	89
	%	27.00%	38.20%	6.70%	14.60%	13.50%	100.00%
Elementary Level	No.	18	29	8	10	8	73
	%	24.70%	39.70%	11.00%	13.70%	11.00%	100.00%
High School Level	No.	3	12	1	3	7	26
	%	11.50%	46.20%	3.80%	11.50%	26.90%	100.00%
Hr. Sec. Level	No.	1	1	1	0	2	5
	%	20.00%	20.00%	20.00%	0.00%	40.00%	100.00%
Total		**46**	**76**	**16**	**26**	**29**	**193**

Source: Compiled with Primary Data

It is proclaimed from the Table 5.15 that out of 89 sanitary workers having no formal education, 27.0 percent of them have strongly agreed to suffering from temporary illness due to the sanitary work whereas 38.2 percent of them have agreed and 6.7 percent of these workers have neither expressed agreement nor disagreement. On the other hand, disagreement was felt by 14.6 percent of these workers and strong disagreement was found among 13.5 percent of such workers.

Among 73 sanitary workers who had their education at the elementary level, 24.7 percent of them have strong agreement about suffering from temporary illness due to the sanitary work whereas 39.7 percent of these workers have agreed and 11.0 percent of them have kept neutrality. About 13.7 percent of them have disagreed and 11.0 percent of these workers have strongly disagreed that they were suffering from temporary illness due to the sanitary work.

In the case of 26 sanitary workers who have completed high school level of education, 11.5 percent of them have strongly agreed and 46.2 percent of them have agreed while 3.8 percent of them were neutral. The proportion of these workers who have disagreed that they were suffering from temporary illness due to the sanitary work was found to be 11.5 percent and that of strongly disagreed sanitary workers was 26.9 per cent.

There were only 5 sanitary workers who have completed higher secondary level education. Among them, 20 percent have strongly agreed that they were suffering from temporary illness due to the sanitary work whereas 20 percent have agreed to this statement and 20 percent have neither agreed nor disagreed. About 40 percent of them have strongly disagreed.

With a view to ensure the above observation, the following hypotheses have been framed and tested:

Null Hypothesis H_0: There is no significant relationship between the educational level and suffering from temporary illness due to the sanitary work

Alternative Hypothesis H_1: There is a significant relationship between the educational level and suffering from temporary illness due to the sanitary work.

Table 5.16: Educational Level and Suffering from Temporary Illness due to Sanitary Work – Chi Square Test

Factor	*Chi square*	*DF*	*p value*	*Result*
Educational Level	11.514	12	0.485	Accepted

According to the Table 5.16, the computed value of chi square and p value indicating the relationship between the educational level and suffering from temporary illness due to the sanitary work were 11.514 and 0.485 respectively. The null hypothesis is accepted as the p value is greater than 0.05. The hypothesis that 'the educational level and suffering from temporary illness due to the sanitary work are not significantly related' holds good. Hence, it is concluded that suffering from temporary illness due to sanitary work is not greater to any specific group of sanitary workers categorized by educational level.

Table 5.17: Monthly Income and Suffering from Temporary Illness due to Sanitary Work

Monthly Income	*Frequency*	*SA*	*A*	*N*	*DA*	*SDA*	*Total*
Below Rs. 6000	No.	3	7	1	3	0	14
	%	21.40%	50.00%	7.10%	21.40%	0.00%	100.00%
Rs.6000 to Rs. 12000	No.	6	16	3	1	3	29
	%	20.70%	55.20%	10.30%	3.40%	10.30%	100.00%
Rs.12000 to Rs. 18000	No.	24	32	9	15	12	92
	%	26.10%	34.80%	9.80%	16.30%	13.00%	100.00%
Above Rs. 18000	No.	13	21	3	7	14	58
	%	22.40%	36.20%	5.20%	12.10%	24.10%	100.00%
Total		**46**	**76**	**16**	**26**	**29**	**193**

Source: Compiled with Primary Data

Table 5.17 reveals that out of 14 sanitary workers earning a monthly income of below Rs.6000, 21.4 percent of them have strongly agreed that they were suffering from temporary illness due to the sanitary work whereas 50 percent of them have agreed and 7.1 percent of them have neither agreed nor disagreed. The proportion of these workers who have disagreed that they were suffering from temporary illness due to the sanitary work was found to be 21.4 per cent.

Among 29 sanitary workers categorized by monthly income as 'Rs.6000 to Rs.12000', the strong disagreement to suffering from temporary illness due to the sanitary work was found among 20.7 percent and agreement was expressed by 55.2 percent of these workers whereas neutral response was given by 10.3 percent of such workers. About 3.4 percent of these workers have disagreed and another 10.3 percent have strongly disagreed that they were suffering from temporary illness due to the sanitary work.

It could be understood that out of 92 sanitary workers categorized under 'Rs.12000 to Rs.18000' monthly income group, 26.1 percent of them have strongly agreed that they were suffering from temporary illness due to the sanitary work whereas 34.8 percent of them agreed and 9.8 percent of these workers expressed neutral opinion. About 16.3 percent of these workers have disagreed and 13 percent of them have strongly disagreed that they were suffering from temporary illness due to the sanitary work.

The results show that out of 58 sanitary workers pertaining to the monthly income group of 'Above Rs.18000', 22.4 percent of them have strongly agreed and 36.2 percent of them have agreed while 5.2 percent of these respondents kept neutrality. Around 12.1 percent of these workers have disagreed and 24.1 percent of such workers have strongly disagreed that they were suffering from temporary illness due to the sanitary work

With a view to examine the relationship between monthly income and suffering from temporary illness due to the sanitary work, the following hypotheses have been framed and tested:

Null Hypothesis H_0: There is no significant relationship between the monthly income and suffering from temporary illness due to the sanitary work.

Alternative Hypothesis H_1: There is a significant relationship between the monthly income and suffering from temporary illness due to the sanitary work.

Table 5.18: Monthly Income and Suffering from Temporary Illness due to Sanitary Work – Chi Square Test

Factor	*Chi square*	*DF*	*p value*	*Result*
Monthly Income	13.802	12	0.314	Accepted

It could be understood that the value of chi square computed to be 13.802 while the p value notifying the relationship between the monthly income and suffering from temporary illness due to the sanitary work was found to be 0.314. Since the p value exceeds 0.05, the null hypothesis is accepted. Thus it could be concluded that the relationship between the monthly income and suffering from temporary illness due to the sanitary work is not significant. It denotes that suffering from temporary illness due to the sanitary work is common to all the sanitary workers grouped by their monthly income.

Table 5.19: Nature of Work and Suffering from Temporary Illness due to Sanitary Work

Nature of Work	*Frequency*	*SA*	*A*	*N*	*DA*	*SDA*	*Total*
Sweeping	No.	17	16	4	7	6	50
	%	34.00%	32.00%	8.00%	14.00%	12.00%	100.00%
Collection	No.	12	35	8	12	17	84
	%	14.30%	41.70%	9.50%	14.30%	20.20%	100.00%
Loading	No.	17	25	4	7	6	59
	%	28.80%	42.40%	6.80%	11.90%	10.20%	100.00%
Total		**46**	**76**	**16**	**26**	**29**	**193**

Source: Compiled with Primary Data.

According to the Table 5.19, out of 50 sweepers, 34 percent have strongly agreed that they were suffering from temporary illness due to the sanitary work whereas 32 percent of these workers have agreed and 8 percent of such workers have responded neutrally. About 14 percent of these workers have disagreed that they were suffering from temporary illness due to the sanitary work whereas 12 percent of sweepers have strongly disagreed that they were suffering from temporary illness due to the sanitary work.

Among 84 garbage collection workers, 14.3 percent expressed strong agreement towards suffering from temporary illness due to the sanitary work whereas 41.7 percent have agreed and 9.5 percent have given neutral response. Around 14.3 percent of these workers have disagreed and 20.2 percent of them have strongly disagreed that they were suffering from temporary illness due to the sanitary work.

Out of 59 sanitary workers engaged in loading of the solid waste, 28.8 percent of them have strongly agreed and 42.4 percent of these workers have agreed that sanitary work has caused temporary illness to them. However, 6.8 percent of them have no opinion about the temporary illness due to the sanitary work. About 11.9 percent of these workers have disagreed and 10.2 percent of such workers have strongly disagreed that they were suffering from temporary illness due to sanitary work.

It could be understood that the agreement was greater among the sweepers and the loading workers while disagreement was higher among the collection workers.

With a view to examine this assertion, the following hypotheses have been framed and tested:

Null Hypothesis H_0: There is no significant relationship between the nature of work and suffering from temporary illness due to the sanitary work

Alternative Hypothesis H_1: There is a significant relationship between the nature of work and suffering from temporary illness due to the sanitary work.

Table 5.20: Nature of Work and Suffering from Temporary Illness due to Sanitary Work – Chi Square Test

Factor	*Chi square*	*DF*	*p value*	*Result*
Nature of Work	10.168	8	0.253	Accepted

From the Table 5.20, it could be realized that the computed value of chi square was 10.168 and the p value measuring the relationship between the nature of work and suffering from temporary illness due to the sanitary work was ascertained to be 0.253. The p value is found to be greater than 0.05 which results in the acceptance of null hypothesis. The conclusion thus drawn from this result is that there is no significant difference in the suffering from temporary illness due to the sanitary work among the selected workers categorized by their nature of work.

Table 5.21: Age and Being Affected by Acute Illness due to the Sanitary Work

Age	*Frequency*	*SA*	*A*	*N*	*DA*	*SDA*	*Total*
Below 25 years	No.	3	13	3	3	2	24
	%	12.50%	54.20%	12.50%	12.50%	8.30%	100.00%
25 to 35 years	No.	15	17	10	8	6	56
	%	26.80%	30.40%	17.90%	14.30%	10.70%	100.00%
35 to 50 years	No.	14	41	10	8	3	76
	%	18.40%	53.90%	13.20%	10.50%	3.90%	100.00%
Above 50 years	No.	7	17	2	10	1	37
	%	18.90%	45.90%	5.40%	27.00%	2.70%	100.00%
Total		**39**	**88**	**25**	**29**	**12**	**193**

Source: Compiled with Primary Data

The opinion i.e. being affected by acute illnesses was agreed by 45.59 percent of the sample workers and strongly agreed by 20.20 percent of sanitary workers. The acute illnesses affecting the sanitary workers include cardiovascular degeneration, musculoskeletal disorders, pulmonary disorders and dermatitis. Their working conditions exposed them to harmful gases such as methane and hydrogen sulphide which make them vulnerable to acute pulmonary diseases. Since they are contacting animal and human discharges frequently they are prone to an acute infection viz. leptospriosis. A study published by the Environmental Information system has also found that the sanitary workers were much vulnerable to acute illnesses.

Table 5.21, it could be understood that out of 24 respondents in the age group of below 25 years, 12.5 percent of them have strongly agreed while 54.2 percent of them have agreed and 12.5 percent of them were neutral. Disagreement was expressed by 12.5 percent of these respondents and strong disagreement was stated by 8.3 percent of these respondents. It reveals that in the age group of below 25 years, the major proportion of the respondents have agreed that they were affected by acute illness due to the sanitary work.

Out of 56 respondents pertaining to the age group of 25 to 35 years, 26.8 percent have strongly agreed whereas 30.4 percent have agreed and 17.9 percent of them have neutral status. Among these respondents 14.3 percent of them have disagreed and 10.7 percent have strongly disagreed. It implies that a major proportion of the respondents belonging to this age group has agreed that they have been affected by acute illness due to the sanitary work.

Among 76 respondents falling under the age group of 35 to 50 years, 18.4 percent of them have strongly agreed while 53.9 percent of them have agreed and neutrality has been maintained by 13.2 percent of such respondents. It is noted that 10.5 percent of these respondents have disagreed and 3.9 percent of them have strongly disagreed. It implies that a majority of the respondents in this group have agreed that they have been affected by acute illness due to the sanitary work.

It is observed that out of 37 respondents belonging to the age group of 'Above 50 years', 18.9 percent of them have strongly agreed whereas 45.9 percent of them have agreed and 5.4 percent of the respondents did not express agreement nor disagreement. Further, there were 27.0 percent of respondents who have disagreed and 2.7 percent of them have strongly disagreed. It denotes that a major proportion of these respondents agreed that they have been affected by acute illness due to the sanitary work.

With a view to understand the significance of relationship between the age of the respondents and their level of agreement to the acute illness due to the sanitary work, the following hypotheses have been framed and tested:

Null Hypothesis H_0: There is no significant relationship between the age of the respondents and suffering from acute illness due to the sanitary work.

Alternative Hypothesis H_1: There is a significant relationship between the age of the respondents and suffering from acute illness due to the sanitary work.

Table 5.22: Age and Being Affected by Acute Illness due to the Sanitary Work – Chi Square Test

Factor	*Chi square*	*DF*	*p value*	*Result*
Age	17.183	12	0.143	Accepted

According to Table 5.22 the computed value of chi square was 17.183 anc, the p value indicating the relationship between the age of the respondents and agreement to injury while performing the sanitary work was found to be 0.143. Since the p value is greater than 0.05, it falls in the acceptance region. Hence, the null hypothesis is accepted and it is concluded that there exists no significant relationship between the age of the sanitary workers and suffering by acute illness due to the sanitary work. It indicates that suffering from acute illness due to the sanitary work is common to all the age groups of the sanitary workers.

Table 5.23: Gender and Being Affected by Acute Illness due to Sanitary Work

Gender	*Frequency*	*SA*	*A*	*N*	*DA*	*SDA*	*Total*
Male	No.	18	36	12	14	5	85
	%	21.20%	42.40%	14.10%	16.50%	5.90%	100.00%
Female	No.	21	52	13	15	7	108
	%	19.40%	48.10%	12.00%	13.90%	6.50%	100.00%
Total		**39**	**88**	**25**	**29**	**12**	**193**

Source: Compiled with Primary Data

It is divulged from the Table 5.23 that out of 85 male respondents, 21.2 percent of them have strongly agreed that they were affected by acute illness due to the sanitary work and 42.4 percent of such respondents have agreed while 14.1 percent of them have neither agreed nor disagreed. Out of these respondents 16.5 percent of them have disagreed and 5.9 percent of them have strongly disagreed that they have got acute illness due to the sanitary work.

Among 108 female workers, 19.4 percent of them have strongly agreed that they have been affected by acute illness due to the sanitary work whereas 48.1 percent of them have agreed and 12 percent of them maintained neutrality. About 13.9 percent of them have disagreed that they were affected by acute illness due to the sanitary work and 6.5 percent of them have strongly disagreed.

In order to understand the significance of the relationship between the age of the sanitary workers and the level of agreement to be affected by acute illness due to the sanitary work, the following hypotheses have been framed and tested:

Null Hypothesis H_0: There is no significant relationship between the gender of the sanitary workers and suffering from acute illness due to the sanitary work.

Alternative Hypothesis H_1: There is a significant relationship between the gender of the sanitary workers and suffering from acute illness due to the sanitary work.

Table 5.24: Gender and Being Affected by Acute Illness due to Sanitary Work – Chi Square Test

Factor	*Chi square*	*DF*	*p value*	*Result*
Gender	0.818	4	0.936	Accepted

It could be revealed from the Table 5.24 that the p value stating the relationship between the gender and level of agreement to suffering from acute illness due to the sanitary work was 0.28. Since the p value is greater than 0.05, it falls in the acceptance region. Hence, the null hypothesis is accepted and it is concluded that there exists no significant relationship between the gender of the sanitary workers and suffering from acute illness due to the sanitary work.

Table 5.25: Educational Level and Being Affected by Acute Illness due to Sanitary Work

Educational Level	*Frequency*	*SA*	*A*	*N*	*DA*	*SDA*	*Total*
No formal education	No.	17	41	10	13	8	89
	%	19.10%	46.10%	11.20%	14.60%	9.00%	100.00%
Elementary Level	No.	16	30	10	14	3	73
	%	21.90%	41.10%	13.70%	19.20%	4.10%	100.00%
High School Level	No.	5	14	5	1	1	26
	%	19.20%	53.80%	19.20%	3.80%	3.80%	100.00%
Hr. Sec. Level	No.	1	3	0	1	0	5
	%	20.00%	60.00%	0.00%	20.00%	0.00%	100.00%
Total		**39**	**88**	**25**	**29**	**12**	**193**

Source: Compiled with Primary Data

Table 5.25 proclaims that out of 89 sanitary workers having no formal education, 19.1 percent of them have strongly agreed to be affected by acute illness due to the sanitary work whereas 46.1 percent have agreed and 11.2 percent of these workers have neither expressed agreement nor disagreement. On the other hand, disagreement was felt by 14.6 percent of these workers and strong disagreement was found among 9 percent of such workers.

Among 73 sanitary workers who had their education at the elementary level, 21.9 percent of them have strong agreement about being affected by acute illness due to the sanitary work whereas 41.1 percent of these workers have agreed and 13.7 percent of them have kept neutrality. About 19.2 percent of them have disagreed and 4.1 percent of these workers have strongly disagreed that they were affected by acute illness due to the sanitary work.

In the case of 26 sanitary workers who have completed high school level of education, 19.2 percent of them have strongly agreed and 53.8 percent of them have agreed while 19.2 percent of them were neutral. The proportion of these workers who have disagreed that they were affected by acute illness due to the sanitary work was found to be 3.8 percent and that of strongly disagreed sanitary workers was 3.8 per cent.

There were only 5 sanitary workers who have completed higher secondary level education. Among them, 20 percent of them have strongly agreed that they were affected by acute illness due to the sanitary work whereas 60 percent of them have agreed to this statement and none of them have neither agreed nor disagreed. About 20 percent of them have disagreed.

With a view to ensure the above observation, the following hypotheses have been framed and tested:

Null Hypothesis H_0: There is no significant relationship between the educational level and suffering from acute illness due to the sanitary work

Alternative Hypothesis H_1: There is a significant relationship between the educational level and suffering from acute illness due to the sanitary work.

Table 5.26: Educational Level and Being Affected by Acute Illness due to the Sanitary Work – Chi Square Test

Factor	*Chi square*	*DF*	*p value*	*Result*
Educational Level	8.049	12	0.781	Accepted

It could be divulged from the Table 5.26 that the computed value of chi square and p value indicating the relationship between the educational level and being affected by acute illness due to the sanitary work were 8.049 and 0.781 respectively. The null hypothesis is accepted as the p value is found to be greater than 0.05. The hypothesis that the educational level and being affected by acute illness due to the sanitary work are not significantly related' holds good. Hence, it is concluded that being affected by acute illness due to the sanitary work is not greater to any specific group of sanitary workers categorized by educational level.

Table 5.27: Monthly Income and Being Affected by Acute Illness due to Sanitary Work

Monthly Income	*Frequency*	*SA*	*A*	*N*	*DA*	*SDA*	*Total*
Below Rs. 6000	No.	4	6	1	3	0	14
	%	28.60%	42.90%	7.10%	21.40%	0.00%	100.00%
Rs.6000 to Rs. 12000	No.	6	15	3	5	0	29
	%	20.70%	51.70%	10.30%	17.20%	0.00%	100.00%
Rs.12000 to Rs. 18000	No.	16	42	14	15	5	92
	%	17.40%	45.70%	15.20%	16.30%	5.40%	100.00%
Above Rs. 18000	No.	13	25	7	6	7	58
	%	22.40%	43.10%	12.10%	10.30%	12.10%	100.00%
Total		**39**	**88**	**25**	**29**	**12**	**193**

Source: Compiled with Primary Data

From the Table 5.27 it is evinced that out of 14 sanitary workers earning a monthly income of below Rs.6000, 28.6 percent of them have strongly agreed that they were affected by acute illness due to the sanitary work whereas 42.9 percent of them have agreed and 7.1 percent of them have neither agreed nor disagreed. The proportion of these workers who have disagreed that they were affected by acute illness due to the sanitary work was found to be 21.4 per cent.

Among 29 sanitary workers categorized by monthly income as 'Rs.6000 to Rs.12000', the strong disagreement to be affected by acute illness due to the sanitary work was found among 20.7 percent and agreement was expressed by 51.7 percent of these workers whereas neutral response was given by 10.3 percent of such workers. About 17.2 percent of these workers have disagreed and none of them have strongly disagreed that they were affected by acute illness due to the sanitary work.

It could be understood that out of 92 sanitary workers categorized under 'Rs.12000 to Rs.18000' monthly income group,17.4 percent of them have strongly agreed that they were affected by acute illness due to the sanitary work whereas 45.7 percent of them were agreed and 15.2 percent of these workers expressed neutral opinion. About 16.3 percent of these workers have disagreed and 5.4 percent of them have strongly disagreed that they were affected by acute illness due to the sanitary work.

The results show that out of 58 sanitary workers pertaining to the monthly income group of 'Above Rs.18000', 22.4 percent of them have strongly agreed and 43.1 percent of them have agreed while 12.1 percent of these respondents kept neutrality. Around 10.3 percent of these workers have disagreed and 12.1 percent of such workers have strongly disagreed that they were affected by acute illness due to the sanitary work

With a view to examine the relationship between monthly income and being affected by acute illness due to the sanitary work, the following hypotheses have been framed and tested:

Null Hypothesis H_0: There is no significant relationship between monthly income and suffering from acute illness due to the sanitary work.

Alternative Hypothesis H_1: There is a significant relationship between the monthly income and suffering from acute illness due to the sanitary work.

Table 5.28: Monthly Income and Being Affected by Acute Illness due to Sanitary Work – Chi Square Test

Factor	*Chi square*	*DF*	*p value*	*Result*
Monthly Income	9.627	12	0.649	Accepted

It could be understood that the value of chi square was computed to be 9.627 while the p value notifying the relationship between monthly income and being affected by acute illness due to the sanitary work was found to be 0.649. Since the p value exceeds 0.05, the null hypothesis is accepted. Thus it could be concluded that the relationship between the monthly income and being affected by acute illness due to sanitary work is not significant. It denotes that being affected by acute illness due to the sanitary work is common to all the sanitary workers grouped by their monthly income.

Table 5.29: Nature of Work and Being Affected by Acute Illness due to Sanitary Work

Monthly Income	*Frequency*	*SA*	*A*	*N*	*DA*	*SDA*	*Total*
Sweeping	No.	14	24	4	6	2	50
	%	28.00%	48.00%	8.00%	12.00%	4.00%	100.00%
Collection	No.	15	36	14	11	8	84
	%	17.90%	42.90%	16.70%	13.10%	9.50%	100.00%
Loading	No.	10	28	7	12	2	59
	%	16.90%	47.50%	11.90%	20.30%	3.40%	100.00%
Total		**39**	**88**	**25**	**29**	**12**	**193**

Source: Compiled with Primary Data

According to the Table 5.29, out of 50 sweepers, 28 percent of them have strongly agreed that they were affected by acute illness due to the sanitary work whereas 48 percent of these workers have agreed and 8 percent of such workers have responded neutrally. About 12 percent of these workers have disagreed that they were affected by acute illness due to the sanitary work whereas 4 percent of sweepers have strongly disagreed that they were affected by acute illness due to the sanitary work.

Among 84 garbage collection workers, 17.9 percent of them expressed strong agreement towards being affected by acute illness due to the sanitary work whereas 42.9 percent of them have agreed and 16.7 percent of them have given neutral response. Around 13.1 percent of these workers have disagreed and 9.5 percent of them have strongly disagreed that they were affected by acute illness due to the sanitary work.

Out of 59 sanitary workers engaged in loading of the solid waste, 16.9 percent of them have strongly agreed and 47.5 percent of these workers have agreed that the sanitary work has caused temporary illness to them. However, 11.9 percent of them have no opinion about the temporary illness due to the sanitary work. About 20.3 percent of these workers have disagreed and 3.4 percent of such workers have strongly disagreed that they were affected by acute illness due to the sanitary work.

It could be understood that the agreement was greater among the sweepers and the loading workers while the disagreement was higher among the collection workers.

With a view to examine this assertion, the following hypotheses have been framed and tested:

Null Hypothesis H_0: There is no significant relationship between the nature of work and being affected by acute illness due to the sanitary work

Alternative Hypothesis H_1: There is a significant relationship between the nature of work and being affected by acute illness due to the sanitary work.

Table 5.30: Nature of Work and Being Affected by Acute Illness due to Sanitary Work – Chi Square Test

Factor	*Chi square*	*DF*	*p value*	*Result*
Nature of Work	8.436	8	0.392	Accepted

From the Table 5.30, it could be realized that the computed value of chi square was 8.436 and the p value measuring the relationship between the nature of work and being affected by acute illness due to the sanitary work was ascertained to be 0.392. The p value is found to be greater than 0.05 which results in the acceptance of null hypothesis. The conclusion thus drawn from this result is that there is no significant difference in being affected by acute illness due to the sanitary work among the selected workers categorized by their nature of work.

Table 5.31: Relationship between Age and Getting Treatment from Government Hospitals

Monthly Income	*Frequency*	*SA*	*A*	*N*	*DA*	*SDA*	*Total*
Below 25 years	No.	5	6	8	3	2	24
	%	20.80%	25.00%	33.30%	12.50%	8.30%	100.00%
25 to 35 years	No.	10	13	12	11	10	56
	%	17.90%	23.20%	21.40%	19.60%	17.90%	100.00%
35 to 50 years	No.	14	19	13	22	8	76
	%	18.40%	25.00%	17.10%	28.90%	10.50%	100.00%
Above 50 years	No.	5	6	3	11	12	37
	%	13.50%	16.20%	8.10%	29.70%	32.40%	100.00%
Total		**34**	**44**	**36**	**47**	**32**	**193**

Source: Compiled with Primary Data

Of the 193 sample sanitary workers, a majority i.e. 24.35 percent disagree the opinion of getting treatment from the government hospitals. They revealed their dissatisfaction about the treatment in the Government hospitals. They prefer private hospitals for the treatment of their chronic illnesses. Around 22.79 percent of sanitary workers agree that they are getting treatment from government hospitals. A good number of sanitary workers due to their meagre income especially those who are working under contract basis prefer only government hospitals.

From the Table 5.31, it could be understood that out of 24 respondents in the age group of below 25 years, 20.8 percent of them have strongly agreed while 25 percent of them have agreed and 33.3 percent of them were neutral. Disagreement was expressed by 12.5 percent of these respondents and strong disagreement was stated by 8.3 percent of these respondents. It reveals that in the age group of below 25 years, a major proportion of the respondents have agreed that they go to the government hospitals for treatment.

Out of 56 respondents pertaining to the age group of 25 to 35 years, 17.9 percent of them have strongly agreed whereas 23.2 percent of them have agreed and 21.4 percent of them have neutral status. Among these respondents 19.6 percent of them have disagreed and 17.9 percent of them have strongly disagreed. It implies that the greatest proportion of the respondents belonging to this age group have agreed that they go to the government hospitals for treatment.

Among 76 respondents falling under the age group of 35 to 50 years, 18.4 percent of them have strongly agreed while 25 percent of them have agreed and neutrality has been maintained by 17.1 percent of such respondents. It is noted that 28.9 percent of these respondents have disagreed and 10.5 percent of them have strongly disagreed. It implies that a majority of the respondents in this group have disagreed that they go to the government hospitals for treatment.

It is observed that out of 37 respondents belonging to the age group of 'Above 50 years', 13.5 percent of them have strongly agreed whereas 16.2 percent of them have agreed and 8.1 percent of the respondents did not express agreement nor disagreement. Further, there were 29.7 percent of respondents who have disagreed and 32.4 percent of them have strongly disagreed. It denotes that a major proportion of these respondents agreed that they always go to the government hospitals for treatment.

With a view to understand the significance of relationship between the age of the respondents and getting treatment from government hospitals, the following hypotheses have been framed and tested:

Null Hypothesis H_0: There is no significant relationship between the age of the respondents and getting treatment from government hospitals for treatment.

Alternative Hypothesis H_1: There is a significant relationship between the age of the respondents and getting treatment from government hospitals for treatment.

Table 5.32: Age and Getting Treatment from Government Hospitals – Chi Square Test

Factor	*Chi square*	*DF*	*p value*	*Result*
Age	18.072	12	0.114	Accepted

According to the Table 5.32 the computed value of chi square was 18.072 and the p value indicating the relationship between the age of the respondents and agreement to go to the government hospitals for treatment was found to be 0.114. Since the p value is greater than 0.05, it falls in the acceptance region. Hence, the null hypothesis is accepted and it is concluded that there exists no significant relationship between the age of the sanitary workers and going to the government hospitals for treatment. It indicates that going to the government hospitals for treatment is common to all the age groups of the sanitary workers.

Table 5.33: Gender and Getting Treatment from Government Hospitals

Gender	*Frequency*	*SA*	*A*	*N*	*DA*	*SDA*	*Total*
Male	No.	12	18	20	20	15	85
	%	14.10%	21.20%	23.50%	23.50%	17.60%	100.00%
Female	No.	22	26	16	27	17	108
	%	20.40%	24.10%	14.80%	25.00%	15.70%	100.00%
Total		**34**	**44**	**36**	**47**	**32**	**193**

Source: Compiled with Primary Data

Table 5.33 portrays that out of 85 male respondents, 14.1 percent of them have strongly agreed that they always go to the government hospital for treatment and 21.2 percent of such respondents have agreed while 23.5 percent of them have neither agreed nor disagreed. Out of these respondents 23.5 percent of them have disagreed and 17.6 percent of them have strongly disagreed that they always go to the government hospital for treatment.

Among 108 female workers, 20.4 percent of them have strongly agreed that they always go to the government hospital for treatment whereas 24.1 percent of them have agreed and 14.8 percent of them maintained neutrality. About 25 percent of them have disagreed that they always go to the government hospital for treatment and 15.7 percent of them have strongly disagreed.

It implies that female workers go to the government hospital for treatment more than male workers.

In order to understand the significance of relationship between the gender of the sanitary workers and their level of agreement regarding getting treatment from government hospitals, the following hypotheses have been framed and tested:

Null Hypothesis H_0: There is no significant relationship between the gender of the sanitary workers and getting treatment from government hospitals.

Alternative Hypothesis H_1: There is a significant relationship between the gender of the sanitary workers and getting treatment from government hospitals.

Table 5.34: Gender and Getting Treatment from Government Hospitals – Chi Square Test

Factor	*Chi square*	*DF*	*p value*	*Result*
Gender	3.314	4	0.507	Accepted

From the Table 5.34, it is observed that the p value stating the relationship between the gender and level of agreement to going to the government hospital for treatment was 3.314. Since the p value is greater than 0.05, it falls in the acceptance region. Hence, the null hypothesis is accepted and it is concluded that there exists no significant relationship between the gender of the sanitary workers and their level of agreement regarding getting treatment from government hospitals.

Table 5.35: Educational Level and Getting Treatment from Government Hospitals

Educational Level	*Frequency*	*SA*	*A*	*N*	*DA*	*SDA*	*Total*
No formal education	No.	16	25	10	26	12	89
	%	18.00%	28.10%	11.20%	29.20%	13.50%	100.00%
Elementary Level	No.	16	16	10	14	17	73
	%	21.90%	21.90%	13.70%	19.20%	23.30%	100.00%
High School Level	No.	1	3	13	6	3	26
	%	3.80%	11.50%	50.00%	23.10%	11.50%	100.00%
Hr. Sec. Level	No.	1	0	3	1	0	5
	%	20.00%	0.00%	60.00%	20.00%	0.00%	100.00%
Total		**34**	**44**	**36**	**47**	**32**	**193**

Source: Compiled with Primary Data

It is divulged from the Table 5.35 that out of 89 sanitary workers having no formal education, 18.0 percent of them have strongly agreed that they go to the government hospital for treatment whereas 28.1 percent of them have agreed and 11.2 percent of these workers have neither expressed agreement nor disagreement. On the other hand, disagreement was felt by 29 percent of these workers and strong disagreement was found among 13.5 percent of such workers.

Among 73 sanitary workers who had their education at the elementary level, 21.9 percent of them have strong agreement about going to the government hospital for treatment whereas 21.9 percent of these workers have agreed and 13.7 percent of them have kept neutrality. About 19.2 percent of them have disagreed and 23.3 percent of these workers have strongly disagreed that they always go to the government hospital for treatment.

In the case of 26 sanitary workers who have completed high school level education, 3.8 percent of them have strongly agreed and 11.5 percent of them have agreed while 50 percent of them were neutral. The proportion of these workers who have disagreed that they always go to the government hospital for treatment was found to be 23.1 percent and that of strongly disagreed sanitary workers was 11.5 per cent.

There were only 5 sanitary workers who have completed higher secondary level education. Among them, 20 percent of them have strongly agreed that injury was caused to them while performing the sanitary work whereas none of them have agreed to this statement and 60 percent of them have neither agreed nor disagreed.

With a view to ensure the above observation, the following hypotheses have been framed and tested:

Null Hypothesis H_0: There is no significant relationship between the educational level and getting treatment from government hospitals.

Alternative Hypothesis H_1: There is a significant relationship between the educational level and getting treatment from government hospitals.

Table 5.36: Educational Level and Getting Treatment from Government Hospitals– Chi Square Test

Factor	*Chi square*	*DF*	*p value*	*Result*
Educational Level	34.602	12	0.001	Rejected

According to the Table 5.36, the computed value of chi square and p value indicating the relationship between the educational level and going to the government hospital for treatment were 34.602 and 0.001 respectively. The null hypothesis is rejected as the p value is found to be greater than 0.05. The hypothesis that 'the educational level and injury while performing the sanitary work are not significantly related' does not hold good. Hence, it is concluded that getting treatment from government hospitals is not greater to any specific group of sanitary workers categorized by educational level.

Table 5.37: Monthly Income and Getting Treatment from Government Hospitals

Monthly Income	*Frequency*	*SA*	*A*	*N*	*DA*	*SDA*	*Total*
Below Rs. 6000	No.	3	4	1	3	3	14
	%	21.40%	28.60%	7.10%	21.40%	21.40%	100.00%
Rs.6000 to Rs. 12000	No.	9	12	4	3	1	29
	%	31.00%	41.40%	13.80%	10.30%	3.40%	100.00%
Rs.12000 to Rs. 18000	No.	14	20	17	21	20	92
	%	15.20%	21.70%	18.50%	22.80%	21.70%	100.00%
Above Rs. 18000	No.	8	8	14	20	8	58
	%	13.80%	13.80%	24.10%	34.50%	13.80%	100.00%
Total		**34**	**44**	**36**	**47**	**32**	**193**

Source: Compiled with Primary Data

Table 5.37 reveals that out of 14 sanitary workers earning a monthly income of below Rs.6000, 21.4 percent of them have strongly agreed that they always go to the government hospital for treatment whereas 28.6 percent of them have agreed and 7.1 percent of them have neither agreed nor disagreed. The proportion of these workers who have disagreed that they always go to the government hospital for treatment was found to be 21.4 percent and that of workers who have strongly disagreed was 21.4 per cent.

Among 29 sanitary workers categorized by monthly income as 'Rs.6000 to Rs.12000', the strong disagreement to going to the government hospital for treatment was found among 31 percent and agreement was expressed by 41.4 percent of these workers whereas neutral response was given by 13.8 percent of such workers. About 10.3 percent of these workers have disagreed and another 3.4 percent have strongly disagreed that they always go to the government hospital for treatment.

It could be understood that out of 92 sanitary workers categorized under 'Rs.12000 to Rs.18000' monthly income group, 15.2 percent of them have strongly agreed that they always go to the government hospital for treatment whereas 21.7 percent of them have agreed and 18.5 percent of these workers expressed neutral opinion. About 22.8 percent of these workers have disagreed and 21.7 percent of them have strongly disagreed that they always go to the government hospital for treatment.

The results show that out of 58 sanitary workers pertaining to the monthly income group of 'Above Rs.18000', 13.8 percent of them have strongly agreed and 13.8 percent of them have agreed while 24.1 percent of these respondents kept neutrality. Around 34.5 percent of these workers have disagreed and 13.8 percent of such workers have strongly disagreed that they always go to the government hospital for treatment.

With a view to examine the relationship between monthly income and getting treatment from government hospitals, the following hypotheses have been framed and tested:

Null Hypothesis H_0: There is no significant relationship between monthly income and getting treatment from government hospitals.

Alternative Hypothesis H_1: There is a significant relationship between monthly income and getting treatment from government hospitals.

Table 5.38: Monthly Income and Getting Treatment from Government Hospitals – Chi Square Test

Factor	*Chi square*	*DF*	*p value*	*Result*
Monthly Income	22.746	12	0.03	Rejected

It could be understood from the Table 5.38 that the value of chi square was computed to be 22.746 while the p value notifying the relationship between monthly income and going to the government hospital for treatment was found to be 0.03. Since the p value is less than 0.01, the null hypothesis is rejected. Thus it could be concluded that the relationship between monthly income and going to the government hospital for treatment is significant at 1 percent level of significance. It denotes that getting treatment from government hospitals varied significantly among the sanitary workers grouped by their monthly income.

Table 5.39: Nature of Work and Getting Treatment from Government Hospitals

Nature of Work	*Frequency*	*SA*	*A*	*N*	*DA*	*SDA*	*Total*
Sweeping	No.	6	18	7	11	8	50
	%	12.00%	36.00%	14.00%	22.00%	16.00%	100.00%
Collection	No.	18	12	21	21	12	84
	%	21.40%	14.30%	25.00%	25.00%	14.30%	100.00%
Loading	No.	10	14	8	15	12	59
	%	16.90%	23.70%	13.60%	25.40%	20.30%	100.00%
Total		**34**	**44**	**36**	**47**	**32**	**193**

Source: Compiled with Primary Data

According to the Table 5.39, out of 50 sweepers, 12 percent of them have strongly agreed that they always go to the government hospital for treatment whereas 36 percent of these workers have agreed and 14 percent of such workers have responded neutrally. About 22 percent of these workers have disagreed that they always go to the government hospital for treatment whereas 16 percent of sweeping workers have strongly disagreed that they always go to the government hospital for treatment.

Among 84 garbage collection workers, 21.4 percent of them expressed strong agreement towards going to the government hospital for treatment whereas 14.3 percent of them have agreed and 25 percent of them have given neutral response. Around 25 percent of these workers have disagreed and 14.3 percent of them have strongly disagreed that they always go to the government hospital for treatment.

Out of 59 sanitary workers engaged in loading of the solid waste, 16.9 percent of them have strongly agreed and 23.7 percent of these workers have agreed that they always go to the government hospital for treatment.

However, 13.6 percent of them have no opinion about going to the government hospital for treatment. About 25.4 percent of these workers have disagreed and 20.3 percent of such workers have strongly disagreed that they always go to the government hospital for treatment.

With a view to examine this assertion, the following hypotheses have been framed and tested:

Null Hypothesis H_0: There is no significant relationship between the nature of work and getting treatment from government hospitals.

Alternative Hypothesis H_1: There is a significant relationship between the nature of work and getting treatment from government hospitals.

Table 5.40: Nature of Work and Getting Treatment from Government Hospitals - Chi Square Test

Factor	*Chi square*	*DF*	*p value*	*Result*
Nature of work	12.269	8	0.14	Accepted

From the Table 5.40, it could be realized that the computed value of chi square was 12.269 and the p value measuring the relationship between the nature of work and going to the government hospital for treatment was ascertained to be 0.14. The p value is found to be greater than 0.05 which results in the acceptance of null hypothesis. The conclusion thus drawn from this result is that there is no significant difference in getting treatment from government hospitals among the selected workers categorized by their nature of work.

Table 5.41: Age and Starting the Sanitary Work in the Very Early Morning

Age	*Frequency*	*SA*	*A*	*N*	*DA*	*SDA*	*Total*
Below 25 years	No.	6	9	3	1	5	24
	%	25.00%	37.50%	12.50%	4.20%	20.80%	100.00%
25 to 35 years	No.	26	13	2	8	7	56
	%	46.40%	23.20%	3.60%	14.30%	12.50%	100.00%

35 to 50 years	No.	28	17	7	12	12	76
	%	36.80%	22.40%	9.20%	15.80%	15.80%	100.00%
Above 50 years	No.	12	5	7	6	7	37
	%	32.40%	13.50%	18.90%	16.20%	18.90%	100.00%
Total		**72**	**44**	**19**	**27**	**31**	**193**

Source: Compiled with Primary Data

Around 37.30 percent of sample sanitary workers have strongly agreed that they had started their work at very early morning followed by 22.79 percent of sanitary workers who agree with the opinion of starting their work in early morning. By rule, all the sanitary workers have to sign in the attendance register by 6.00 am every morning, after that they will be assigned areas to cover.

From the Table 5.41, it could be understood that out of 24 respondents in the age group of below 25 years, 25 percent of them have strongly agreed while 37.5 percent of them have agreed and 12.5 percent of them were neutral. Disagreement was expressed by 4.2 percent of these respondents and strong disagreement was stated by 20.8 percent of these respondents. It reveals that in the age group of below 25 years, a major proportion of the respondents have agreed that they start the sanitary work in the very early morning.

Out of 56 respondents pertaining to the age group of 25 to 35 years, 46.4 percent of them have strongly agreed whereas 23.2 percent of them have agreed and 3.6 percent of them have neutral status. Among these respondents 14.3 percent of them have disagreed and 12.5 percent of them have strongly disagreed. It implies that a major proportion of the respondents belonging to this age group have agreed that they start the sanitary work in the very early morning.

Among 76 respondents falling under the age group of 35 to 50 years, 36.8 percent of them have strongly agreed while 22.4 percent of them have agreed and neutrality has been maintained by 9.2 percent of such respondents. It is noted that 15.8 percent of these respondents have disagreed and 15.8 percent of them have strongly disagreed. It implies that a majority of the respondents in this group have agreed that they start sanitary work in the very early morning.

It is observed that out of 37 respondents belonging to the age group of 'Above 50 years', 32.4 percent of them have strongly agreed whereas 13.5 percent of them have agreed and 18.9 percent of the respondents did not express agreement nor disagreement. Further, there were 16.2 percent of respondents who have disagreed and 18.9 percent of them have strongly disagreed. It denotes that a major proportion of these respondents agreed that they start the sanitary work in the very early morning.

With a view to understand the significance of relationship between the age of the respondents and their level of agreement to start the sanitary work in the very early morning, the following hypotheses have been framed and tested:

Null Hypothesis H_0: There is no significant relationship between the age of the respondents and their level of agreement to start the sanitary work in the very early morning.

Alternative Hypothesis H_1: There is a significant relationship between the age of the respondents and their level of agreement to start the sanitary work in the very early morning.

Table 5.42: Age and Starting the Sanitary Work in the Very Early Morning – Chi Square Test

Factor	*Chi square*	*DF*	*p value*	*Result*
Age	14.625	12	0.263	Accepted

Table 5.42 evinces that the computed value of chi square was 14.625 and the p value indicating the relationship between the age of the respondents and agreement to starting the sanitary work in the very early morning was found to be 0.263. Since the p value is greater than 0.05, it falls in the acceptance region. Hence, the null hypothesis

is accepted and it is concluded that there exists no significant relationship between the age of the sanitary workers and starting the sanitary work in the very early morning. It indicates that starting the sanitary work in the very early morning is common to all groups of the sanitary workers.

Table 5.43: Gender and Starting Sanitary Work in the Very Early Morning

Gender	*Frequency*	*SA*	*A*	*N*	*DA*	*SDA*	*Total*
Male	No.	24	19	14	11	17	85
	%	28.20%	22.40%	16.50%	12.90%	20.00%	100.00%
Female	No.	48	25	5	16	14	108
	%	44.40%	23.10%	4.60%	14.80%	13.00%	100.00%
Total		**72**	**44**	**19**	**27**	**31**	**193**

Source: Compiled with Primary Data

Table 5.43 evinces that out of 85 male respondents, 28.2 percent of them have strongly agreed that they start the sanitary work in the very early morning and 22.4 percent of such respondents have agreed while 16.5 percent of them have neither agreed nor disagreed. Out of these respondents 12.9 percent of them have disagreed and 20 percent of them have strongly disagreed that they start the sanitary work in the very early morning.

Among 108 female workers, 44.4 percent of them have strongly agreed that they start the sanitary work in the very early morning whereas 23.1 percent of them have agreed and 4.6 percent of them maintained neutrality. About 14.8 percent of them have disagreed that they start the sanitary work in the very early morning and 13 percent of them have strongly disagreed.

It implies that female workers have to start the sanitary work in the very early morning. In order to understand the significance of relationship between the gender of the sanitary workers and the level of agreement to start the sanitary work in the early morning, the following hypotheses have been framed and tested:

Null Hypothesis H_0: There is no significant relationship between the gender of the sanitary workers and their level of agreement to start the sanitary work in the very early morning.

Alternative Hypothesis H_1: There is a significant relationship between the gender of the sanitary workers and their level of agreement to start the sanitary work in the very early morning.

Table 5.44: Gender and Starting the Sanitary Work in the Very Early Morning – Chi Square Test

Factor	*Chi square*	*DF*	*p value*	*Result*
Gender	11.723	4	0.02	Rejected

From the Table 5.44, it is observed that the p value stating the relationship between the gender and level of agreement to start the sanitary work in the very early morning was 0.02. Since the p value is less than 0.05, it falls in the rejection region.

Hence, the null hypothesis is rejected and it is concluded that there exists a significant relationship between the gender of the sanitary workers and their level of agreement to start the sanitary work in the very early morning.

Table 5.45: Educational Level and Starting Sanitary Work in the Very Early Morning

Educational Level	*Frequency*	*SA*	*A*	*N*	*DA*	*SDA*	*Total*
No formal education	No.	41	14	7	10	17	89
	%	46.10%	15.70%	7.90%	11.20%	19.10%	100.00%
Elementary Level	No.	24	19	9	11	10	73
	%	32.90%	26.00%	12.30%	15.10%	13.70%	100.00%
High School Level	No.	6	10	2	4	4	26
	%	23.10%	38.50%	7.70%	15.40%	15.40%	100.00%
Hr. Sec. Level	No.	1	1	1	2	0	5
	%	20.00%	20.00%	20.00%	40.00%	0.00%	100.00%
Total		**72**	**44**	**19**	**27**	**31**	**193**

Source: Compiled with Primary Data

It is divulged from the Table 5.45 that out of 89 sanitary workers having no formal education, 46.1 percent of them have strongly agreed to start the sanitary work in the very early morning whereas 15.7 percent of them have agreed and 7.9 percent of these workers have neither expressed agreement nor disagreement. On the other hand, disagreement was felt by 11.2 percent of these workers and strong disagreement was found among 19.1 percent of such workers.

Among 73 sanitary workers who had their education at the elementary level, 32.9 percent of them have strong agreement about starting the sanitary work in the very early morning whereas 26 percent of these workers have agreed and 12.3 percent of them have kept neutrality. About 15.1 percent of them have disagreed and 13.7 percent of these workers have strongly disagreed that they start the sanitary work in the very early morning.

In the case of 26 sanitary workers who have completed high school level education, 23.1 percent of them have strongly agreed and 38.5 percent of them have agreed while 7.7 percent of them were neutral. The proportion of these workers who have disagreed to start the sanitary work in the very early morning was found to be 15.4 percent and that of strongly disagreed sanitary workers was 15.4 per cent.

There were only 5 sanitary workers who have completed higher secondary level education. Among them, 20 percent of them have strongly agreed that they start the sanitary work in the very early morning whereas 20 percent of them have agreed to this statement and 20 percent of them have neither agreed nor disagreed. About 40 percent of these workers have disagreed that they start the sanitary work in the very early morning.

With a view to ensure the above observation, the following hypotheses have been framed and tested:

Null Hypothesis H_0: There is no significant relationship between the educational level and agreement to start the sanitary work in the very early morning.

Alternative Hypothesis H_1: There is a significant relationship between the educational level and agreement to start the sanitary work in the very early morning.

Table 5.46: Educational Level and Starting the Sanitary Work in the Very Early Morning – Chi Square Test

Factor	*Chi square*	*DF*	*p value*	*Result*
Educational Level	15.158	12	0.233	Accepted

According to the Table 5.46, the computed value of chi square and p value indicating the relationship between the educational level and starting the sanitary work in the very early morning were 15.158 and 0.233 respectively. The null hypothesis is accepted as the p value is found to be greater than 0.05. The hypothesis that 'the educational level and starting the sanitary work in the very early morning are not significantly related' holds good. Hence, it is concluded that starting the sanitary work in the very early morning is not greater to any specific group of sanitary workers categorized by educational level.

Table 5.47: Monthly Income and Starting the Sanitary Work in the Very Early Morning

Monthly Income	*Frequency*	*SA*	*A*	*N*	*DA*	*SDA*	*Total*
Below Rs. 6000	No.	5	3	2	2	2	14
	%	35.70%	21.40%	14.30%	14.30%	14.30%	100.00%
Rs.6000 to Rs. 12000	No.	14	6	1	4	4	29
	%	48.30%	20.70%	3.40%	13.80%	13.80%	100.00%
Rs.12000 to Rs. 18000	No.	37	21	10	9	15	92
	%	40.20%	22.80%	10.90%	9.80%	16.30%	100.00%
Above Rs. 18000	No.	16	14	6	12	10	58
	%	27.60%	24.10%	10.30%	20.70%	17.20%	100.00%
Total		**72**	**44**	**19**	**27**	**31**	**193**

Source: Compiled with Primary Data

Table 5.47 depicts that out of 14 sanitary workers earning a monthly income of below Rs.6000, 35.7 percent of them have strongly agreed that they start the sanitary work in the very early morning whereas 21.4 percent of them have agreed and 14.3 percent of them have neither agreed nor disagreed. The proportion of these workers who have disagreed to start the sanitary work in the very early morning was 14.3 percent and that of strongly disagreed workers was found to be 14.3 per cent.

Among 29 sanitary workers categorized by monthly income as 'Rs.6000 to Rs.12000', the strong disagreement to start the sanitary work in the very early morning was found among 48.3 percent and agreement was expressed by 20.7 percent of these workers whereas neutral response was given by 3.4 percent of such workers. About 13.8 percent of these workers have disagreed and another 13.8 percent have strongly disagreed that they started the sanitary work in the very early morning.

It could be understood that out of 92 sanitary workers categorized under 'Rs.12000 to Rs.18000' monthly income group, 40.2 percent of them have strongly agreed that they started the sanitary work in the very early morning whereas 22.8 percent of them were agreed and 10.9 percent of these workers expressed neutral opinion. About 9.8 percent of these workers have disagreed and 16.3 percent of them have strongly disagreed that they started the sanitary work in the very early morning.

The results show that out of 58 sanitary workers pertaining to the monthly income group of 'Above Rs.18000', 27.6 percent of them have strongly agreed and 24.1 percent of them have agreed while 10.3 percent of these respondents kept neutrality. Around 20.7 percent of these workers have disagreed and 17.2 percent of such workers have strongly disagreed that they started the sanitary work in the very early morning.

With a view to examine the relationship between the monthly income and starting the work in the very early morning the following hypotheses have been framed and tested:

Null Hypothesis H_0: There is no significant relationship between the monthly income and agreement to start the sanitary work in the very early morning.

Alternative Hypothesis H_1: There is a significant relationship between the monthly income and agreement to start the sanitary work in the very early morning.

Table 5.48: Monthly Income and Starting Sanitary Work in the Very Early Morning – Chi Square Test

Factor	*Chi square*	*DF*	*p value*	*Result*
Monthly Income	7.536	12	0.82	Accepted

It is proclaimed from the Table 5.48 that the value of chi square was computed to be 7.536 while the p value notifying the relationship between the monthly income and injury while performing sanitary work was found to be 0.82. Since the p value exceeds 0.05, the null hypothesis is accepted. Thus it could be concluded that the relationship between the monthly income and starting the sanitary work in the very early morning is not significant. It denotes that starting the sanitary in the very early morning is common to all the sanitary workers grouped by their monthly income.

Table 5.49: Nature of Work and Starting Sanitary Work in The Very Early Morning

Nature of Work	*Frequency*	*SA*	*A*	*N*	*DA*	*SDA*	*Total*
Sweeping	No.	18	7	5	10	10	50
	%	36.00%	14.00%	10.00%	20.00%	20.00%	100.00%
Collection	No.	37	21	6	8	12	84
	%	44.00%	25.00%	7.10%	9.50%	14.30%	100.00%
Loading	No.	17	16	8	9	9	59
	%	28.80%	27.10%	13.60%	15.30%	15.30%	100.00%
Total		**72**	**44**	**19**	**27**	**31**	**193**

Source: Compiled with Primary Data

It is evinced from the Table 5.49 that out of 50 sweepers, 36 percent of them have strongly agreed that they started the sanitary work in the very early morning whereas 14 percent of these workers have agreed and 10 percent of such workers have responded neutrally. About 20 percent of these workers have disagreed that they started the sanitary work in the very early morning whereas 20 percent of sweepers have strongly disagreed that they started the sanitary work in the very early morning.

Among 84 garbage collection workers, 44 percent of them expressed strong agreement towards starting sanitary work in the very early morning whereas 25 percent of them have agreed and 7.1 percent of them have given neutral response. Around 9.5 percent of these workers have disagreed and 14.3 percent of them have strongly disagreed that they started the sanitary work in the very early morning.

Out of 59 sanitary workers engaged in loading of the solid waste, 28.8 percent of them have strongly agreed and 27.1 percent of these workers have agreed that they started the sanitary work in the very early morning. However, 13.6 percent of them have no opinion about starting the sanitary work in the very early morning. About 15.3 percent of these workers have disagreed and another 15.3 percent of such workers have strongly disagreed that they started the sanitary work in the very early morning.

With a view to examine this assertion, the following hypotheses have been framed and tested:

Null Hypothesis H_0: There is no significant relationship between the nature of work and starting the sanitary work in the very early morning.

Alternative Hypothesis H_1: There is a significant relationship between the nature of work and starting the sanitary work in the very early morning.

Table 5.50: Nature of Work and Starting Sanitary Work in the Very Early Morning – Chi Square Test

Factor	*Chi square*	*DF*	*p value*	*Result*
Nature of work	9.225	8	0.324	Accepted

It could be proclaimed from the Table 5.50 that the computed value of chi square was 9.225 and the p value measuring the relationship between the nature of work and starting the sanitary work in the very early morning was ascertained to be 0.324. The p value is found to be greater than 0.05 which results in the acceptance of null hypothesis. The conclusion thus drawn from this result is that there is no significant difference in starting the sanitary work in the very early morning among the selected workers categorized by their nature of work.

Table 5.51: Age and Excessive Workload

Age	*Frequency*	*SA*	*A*	*N*	*DA*	*SDA*	*Total*
Below 25 years	No.	1	15	4	3	1	24
	%	4.20%	62.50%	16.70%	12.50%	4.20%	100.00%
25 to 35 years	No.	9	32	5	5	5	56
	%	16.10%	57.10%	8.90%	8.90%	8.90%	100.00%
35 to 50 years	No.	15	40	8	3	10	76
	%	19.70%	52.60%	10.50%	3.90%	13.20%	100.00%
Above 50 years	No.	4	19	4	2	8	37
	%	10.80%	51.40%	10.80%	5.40%	21.60%	100.00%
Total		**29**	**106**	**21**	**13**	**24**	**193**

Source: Compiled with Primary Data

Around 54.92 percent of sample sanitary workers agree that they were given over work burden. The workers feel that they were given additional workloads during festivals, Government meetings and natural calamities.

From the Table 5.51, it could be understood that out of 24 respondents in the age group of below 25 years, 4.2 percent of them have strongly agreed while 62.5 percent of them have agreed and 16.7 percent of them were neutral.

Disagreement was expressed by 12.5 percent of these respondents and strong disagreement was stated by 4.2 percent of these respondents. It reveals that in the age group of below 25 years, a major proportion of the respondents have agreed that they were given over workload.

Out of 56 respondents pertaining to the age group of 25 to 35 years, 16.1 percent of them have strongly agreed whereas 57.1 percent of them have agreed and 8.9 percent of them have neutral status. Among these respondents 8.9 percent of them have disagreed and 8.9 percent of them have strongly disagreed. It implies that a major proportion of the respondents belonging to this age group have agreed that they have been given over workload.

Among 76 respondents falling under the age group of 35 to 50 years, 19.7 percent of them have strongly agreed while 52.6 percent of them have agreed and neutrality has been maintained by 10.5 percent of such respondents. It is noted that 3.9 percent of these respondents have disagreed and 13.2 percent of them have strongly disagreed. It implies that a majority of the respondents in this group have agreed that they have been given over workload.

It is observed that out of 37 respondents belonging to the age group of 'Above 50 years', 10.8 percent of them have strongly agreed whereas 51.4 percent of them have agreed and 10.8 percent of the respondents did not express agreement nor disagreement. Further, there were 5.4 percent of respondents who have disagreed and 21.6 percent of them have strongly disagreed. It denotes that a major proportion of these respondents agreed that they have been given over workload.

With a view to understand the significance of the relationship between the age of the respondents and their level of agreement regarding excessive workload, the following hypotheses have been framed and tested:

Null Hypothesis H_0: There is no significant relationship between the age of the respondents and their level of agreement to excessive workload.

Alternative Hypothesis H_1: There is a significant relationship between the age of the respondents and their level of agreement to excessive workload.

Table 5.52: Age and Excessive Workload – Chi Square Test

Factor	*Chi square*	*DF*	*p value*	*Result*
Age	11.862	12	0.457	Accepted

Table 5.52 evinces that the computed value of chi square was 11.862 and the p value indicating the relationship between the age of the respondents and agreement to over workload was found to be 0.457. Since the p value is greater than 0.05, it falls in the acceptance region. Hence, the null hypothesis is accepted and it is concluded that there exists no significant relationship between the age of the sanitary workers and excessive workload. It indicates that excessive workload is common to the various age groups of sanitary workers.

Table 5.53: Gender and Excessive Workload

Gender	*Frequency*	*SA*	*A*	*N*	*DA*	*SDA*	*Total*
Male	No.	14	45	7	7	12	85
	%	16.50%	52.90%	8.20%	8.20%	14.10%	100.00%
Female	No.	15	61	14	6	12	108
	%	13.90%	56.50%	13.00%	5.60%	11.10%	100.00%
Total		**29**	**106**	**21**	**13**	**24**	**193**

Source: Compiled with Primary Data

Table 5.53 portrays that out of 85 male respondents, 16.5 percent of them have strongly agreed that they were given over workload and 52.9 percent of such respondents have agreed while 8.2 percent of them have neither agreed nor disagreed. Out of these respondents 8.2 percent of them have disagreed and 14.1 percent of them have strongly disagreed that they have been given over workload.

Among 108 female workers, 13.9 percent of them have strongly agreed that they have been given over workload whereas 56.5 percent of them have agreed and 13 percent of them maintained neutrality. About 5.6 percent of them have disagreed that they were given over workload and 11.1 percent of them have strongly disagreed.

It implies that female workers were given excessive workload more than male workers.

In order to understand the significance of the relationship between the age of the sanitary workers and the level of agreement to excessive workload, the following hypotheses have been framed and tested:

Null Hypothesis H_0: There is no significant relationship between the age of the sanitary workers and their level of agreement to excessive workload.

Alternative Hypothesis H_1: There is a significant relationship between the age of the sanitary workers and their level of agreement to excessive workload.

Table 5.54: Gender and Excessive Workload – Chi Square Test

Factor	*Chi square*	*DF*	*p value*	*Result*
Gender	2.149	4	0.708	Accepted

From the Table 5.54, it is observed that the p value stating the relationship between the gender and level of agreement to excessive workload was 0.708. Since the p value is greater than 0.05, it falls in the acceptance region. Hence, the null hypothesis is accepted and it is concluded that there exists no significant relationship between the gender of the sanitary workers and their level of agreement to excessive workload.

Table 5.55: Educational Level and Excessive Workload

Educational Level	*Frequency*	*SA*	*A*	*N*	*DA*	*SDA*	*Total*
No formal education	No.	15	47	7	8	12	89
	%	16.90%	52.80%	7.90%	9.00%	13.50%	100.00%

Elementary Level	No.	9	48	10	3	3	73
	%	12.30%	65.80%	13.70%	4.10%	4.10%	100.00%
High School Level	No.	3	11	4	1	7	26
	%	11.50%	42.30%	15.40%	3.80%	26.90%	100.00%
Hr. Sec. Level	No.	2	0	0	1	2	5
	%	40.00%	0.00%	0.00%	20.00%	40.00%	100.00%
Total		**29**	**106**	**21**	**13**	**24**	**193**

Source: Compiled with Primary Data

It is proclaimed from the Table 5.55 that out of 89 sanitary workers having no formal education, 16.9 percent of them have strongly agreed that they were given excessive workload whereas 52.8 percent of them have agreed and 7.9 percent of these workers have neither expressed agreement nor disagreement. On the other hand, disagreement was felt by 9 percent of these workers and strong disagreement was found among 13.5 percent of such workers.

Among 73 sanitary workers who had their education at the elementary level, 12.3 percent of them have strong agreement about over workload whereas 65.8 percent of these workers have agreed and 13.7 percent of them have kept neutrality. About 4.1 percent of them have disagreed and 4.1 percent of these workers have strongly disagreed that they were given over workload.

In the case of 26 sanitary workers who have completed high school level education, 11.5 percent of them have strongly agreed and 42.3 percent of them have agreed while 15.4 percent of them were neutral. The proportion of these workers who have disagreed that they were given over workload was found to be 3.8 percent and that of strongly disagreed sanitary workers was 26.9 per cent.

There were only 5 sanitary workers who have completed the higher secondary level education. Among them, 40 percent of them have strongly agreed that they were given over workload whereas none of them have agreed to this statement and none of them have neither agreed nor disagreed. About 20 percent of them have disagreed and 40 percent of them have strongly disagreed that they were given over workload.

With a view to ensure the above observation, the following hypotheses have been framed and tested:

Null Hypothesis H_0: There is no significant relationship between the educational level and agreement to excessive workload.

Alternative Hypothesis H_1: There is a significant relationship between the educational level and agreement to excessive workload.

Table 5.56: Educational Level and Excessive Workload– Chi Square Test

Factor	*Chi square*	*DF*	*p value*	*Result*
Educational Level	24.912	12	0.015	Rejected

According to the Table 5.56, the computed value of chi square and p value indicating the relationship between the educational level and over workload were 24.912 and 0.015 respectively. The null hypothesis is rejected as the p value is found to be lesser than 0.05. The hypothesis that 'the educational level and suffering from temporary illness due to sanitary work are not significantly related' does not hold good. Hence, it is concluded that excessive workload, varied among the various groups of sanitary workers categorized by educational level.

Table 5.57: Monthly Income and Excessive Workload

Monthly Income	*Frequency*	*SA*	*A*	*N*	*DA*	*SDA*	*Total*
Below Rs.6000	No.	3	6	3	0	2	14
	%	21.40%	42.90%	21.40%	0.00%	14.30%	100.00%
Rs.6000 to Rs.12000	No.	8	14	3	2	2	29
	%	27.60%	48.30%	10.30%	6.90%	6.90%	100.00%
Rs.12000 to Rs.18000	No.	7	57	9	8	11	92
	%	7.60%	62.00%	9.80%	8.70%	12.00%	100.00%

Above Rs.18000	No.	11	29	6	3	9	58
	%	19.00%	50.00%	10.30%	5.20%	15.50%	100.00%
Total		**29**	**106**	**21**	**13**	**24**	**193**

Source: Compiled with Primary Data

Table 5.57 reveals that out of 14 sanitary workers earning a monthly income of below Rs.6000, 21.4 percent of them have strongly agreed that they were given over workload whereas 42.9 percent of them have agreed and 21.4 percent of them have neither agreed nor disagreed. The proportion of these workers who have strongly disagreed that they were given over workload was found to be 14.3 per cent.

Among 29 sanitary workers categorized by monthly income as 'Rs.6000 to Rs.12000', the strong disagreement to over workload was found among 27.6 percent and agreement was expressed by 48.3 percent of these workers whereas neutral response was given by 10.3 percent of such workers. About 6.9 percent of these workers have disagreed and another 6.9 percent have strongly disagreed that they were given over workload.

It could be understood that out of 92 sanitary workers categorized under 'Rs.12000 to Rs.18000' monthly income group, 7.6 percent of them have strongly agreed that they were given over workload whereas 62 percent of them were agreed and 9.8 percent of these workers expressed neutral opinion. About 8.7 percent of these workers have disagreed and 12 percent of them have strongly disagreed that they were given over workload.

The results show that out of 58 sanitary workers pertaining to the monthly income group of 'Above Rs.18000', 19 percent of them have strongly agreed and 50 percent of them have agreed while 10.3 percent of these respondents kept neutrality. Around 5.2 percent of these workers have disagreed and 15.5 percent of such workers have strongly disagreed that they were given over workload.

With a view to examine the relationship between the monthly income and excessive workload, the following hypotheses have been framed and tested:

Null Hypothesis H_0: There is no significant relationship between the monthly income and agreement to excessive workload.

Alternative Hypothesis H_1: There is a significant relationship between the monthly income and agreement to excessive workload.

Table 5.58: Monthly Income and Excessive Workload – Chi Square Test

Factor	*Chi square*	*DF*	*p value*	*Result*
Monthly Income	13.533	12	0.332	Accepted

It could be understood from the Table 5.58 that the value of chi square was computed to be 13.533 while the p value notifying the relationship between the monthly income and excessive workload was found to be 0.332. Since the p value exceeds 0.05, the null hypothesis is accepted. Thus it could be concluded that the relationship between the monthly income and over workload is not significant. It denotes that excessive workload is commonly given to all the sanitary workers grouped by their monthly income.

Table 5.59: Nature of Work and Excessive Workload

Monthly Income	*Frequency*	*SA*	*A*	*N*	*DA*	*SDA*	*Total*
Sweeping	No.	9	27	6	1	7	50
	%	18.00%	54.00%	12.00%	2.00%	14.00%	100.00%
Collection	No.	9	48	10	6	11	84
	%	10.70%	57.10%	11.90%	7.10%	13.10%	100.00%
Loading	No.	11	31	5	6	6	59
	%	18.60%	52.50%	8.50%	10.20%	10.20%	100.00%
Total		**29**	**106**	**21**	**13**	**24**	**193**

Source: Compiled with Primary Data

According to the Table 5.59, out of 50 sweepers, 18 percent of them have strongly agreed that they were given over workload whereas 54 percent of these workers have agreed and 12 percent of such workers have responded neutrally. About 2 percent of these workers have disagreed that they were given over workload whereas 14 percent of sweepers have strongly disagreed that they were given over workload.

Among 84 garbage collection workers, 10.7 percent of them expressed strong agreement towards over workload whereas 57.1 percent of them have agreed and 11.9 percent of them have given neutral response. Around 7.1 percent of these workers have disagreed and 13.1 percent of them have strongly disagreed that they were given over workload.

Out of 59 sanitary workers engaged in loading of the solid waste, 18.6 percent of them have strongly agreed and 52.5 percent of these workers have agreed that they were given over workload. However, 8.5 percent of them have no opinion about the over workload. About 10.2 percent of these workers have disagreed and another 10.2 percent of such workers have strongly disagreed that they were given over workload.

It could be understood that the agreement was greater among the sweepers and the loading workers while disagreement was higher among the collection workers.

With a view to examine this assertion, the following hypotheses have been framed and tested:

Null Hypothesis H_0: There is no significant relationship between the nature of work and excessive workload

Alternative Hypothesis H_1: There is a significant relationship between the nature of work and excessive workload.

Table 5.60: Nature of Work and Excessive Workload – Chi Square Test

Factor	*Chi square*	*DF*	*p value*	*Result*
Nature of work	5.534	8	0.699	Accepted

From the Table 5.60, it could be realized that the computed value of chi square was 5.534 and the p value measuring the relationship between the nature of work and over workload was ascertained to be 0.699. The p value is found to be greater than 0.05 which results in the acceptance of null hypothesis. The conclusion thus drawn from this result is that there is no significant difference in the over workload given to the sanitary workers categorized by their nature of work.

5.2 Health Care Status of Sanitary Workers

Table 5.61: Relationship between Nature of Work and Occupational Health Hazards

Nature of Work	*Occupational Health Hazards Faced*		*Total*
	Yes	*No*	
Sweeping	43	7	50
Collection	77	7	84
Loading	53	6	59
Total	**173**	**20**	**193**

Source: Compiled with Primary Data

Table 5.62: Relationship between Nature of Work and Occupational Health Hazards - Anova

	Sum Squares	*Df*	*Mean Square*	*F*	*Sig*
Between Groups	.101	2	.050	.538	.585
Within Groups	17.826	190	.094		
Total	**17.927**	**192**			

H_0 = There is no significant difference in the occupational health hazards among the different nature of sanitary work.

Of the 193 sanitary workers, a majority i.e. 89.64 percent have been affected by any one of occupational ailments viz. skin problems, occupational injuries, chest pain, respiratory infections, eye problems, bacterial, viral and fungal infections and musculoskeletal disorders. They have been affected both by temporary and chronic illnesses. The major health ailments affecting the sanitary workers include cardiovascular degeneration, infections like hepatitis and laptospirosis, skin problems and respiratory problems (Rajnarayan R. Tiwari, 2008). The sanitary workers reveal that they were affected by contagious diseases and infections, when they are allotted to do scavenging work at cyclone affected areas. Similarly while doing sewage and public toilet cleaning work, they were affected by severe bacterial infections. Regarding the occupational health hazards there exists no significant difference among the sanitary workers engaged in different nature of work viz. sweeping, collection, loading and disposal of waste, since the p value is greater than 0.001. It implies that all types of sanitation work were equally infectious in causing ailments unless safeguarded with sanitary equipments. The sanitary workers should be given awareness about the potential risk of their sanitation work to reduce their occupational health risks. The preventive measures should be taught to them to reduce their risk. Up to date vaccination should be given to them against typhoid fever, Hepatitis A and B.

Table 5.63: Methods of Medication Followed

Methods of Medication	*Frequency*	*Percent*
Self medication	64	33.2
Allopathic Treatment	96	49.7
Non – Allopathic Treatment	33	17.1
Total	**193**	**100.0**

Source: Compiled with Primary Data

Regarding the methods of medical treatment preferred, around 49.7 percent mostly prefer allopathic medicine for their treatment both from Government and private hospitals. Nearly 33.2 percent of sanitary workers mostly adopt self medication to treat their illnesses. It reveals their unawareness about the ill effects of self medication. Due to their meager income and to avoid getting leave for going to hospitals for treatment in order to get wages, many workers working on contract basis as daily wage earners prefer self medication as their mode of treatment. Only 17.1 percent of sanitary workers prefer non – allopathic treatment methods such as ayurveda, unani, yoga, siddha and homeopathy.

Table 5.64: Relationship between Usage of Sanitary Materials and Occupational Health Hazards

Usage of Sanitary Material	*Occupational Health Hazards Faced*		*Total*
	Yes	*No*	
Yes	9	17	26
No	164	3	167
Total	**173**	**20**	**193**

Source: Compiled with Primary Data

Table 5.65: Relationship between Usage of Sanitary Materials and Occupational Health Hazards - Anova

	Sum Squares	*Df*	*Mean Square*	*F*	*Sig*
Between Groups	9.097	1	9.097	196.754	.000
Within Groups	8.831	191	.046		
Total	**17.927**	**192**			

H_0 = There is no significant difference between the health conditions of sanitary workers those who are using and not using sanitary materials.

Though all the sanitary workers were provided sanitary materials viz. gloves, boots, brooms, collection plates, a majority (86.52 per cent) failed to use those materials due to their discomfort in using those materials and unawareness about its usage. The workers also reveal that due to the poo, quality of sanitary materials they were provided, they failed to use those worn out materials. The above analysis reveals that there is a significant difference in the health conditions of sanitary workers who were using and not using the sanitary materials ($p < 0.001$). The sanitary workers who are properly using the sanitary materials were found to be less affected by occupational health hazards. Thus awareness should be given to sanitary workers to use the sanitary materials to avoid infections and diseases. The good quality sanitary materials like waterproof gloves, rubber boots, protective face mask and goggles for eye protection should be distributed to the sanitary workers.

Table 5.66: Relationship between Annual Medical Expenditure and Occupational Health Hazards

Medical Expenses	*Occupational Health Hazards*	
	Yes	*No*
<5000	17	11
5001 – 25000	131	9
25001 – 50000	21	0
50001 - 100000	2	0
>100001	2	0
Total	**173**	**20**

Source: Compiled with Primary Data

Table 5.67: Relationship between Annual Medical Expenditure and Occupational Health Hazards - Anova

	Sum of Squares	*Df*	*Mean Square*	*F*	*Sig*
Between Groups	17.232	4	4.308	14.032	.000
Within Groups	57.721	188	.307		
Total	**74.953**	**192**			

A significant difference is observed between the medical expenses incurred by the sanitary workers affected by occupational health hazards and those who were unaffected ($p<0.001$). The sanitary workers facing occupational health hazards were found to incur a large amount of medical expenses when compared to others. The following analysis reveals that among the category of affected workers those who are obtaining treatment from Government hospitals incur a lesser amount of medical expenses than those who are getting treatment from private clinics and hospitals. The results have been obtained from the opinion revealed by the sanitary workers regarding their mode of treatment shown below.

This chapter attempted to analyze the occupational health status and health care practices of the sanitary workers in Salem Corporation. It was found that a majority of the sanitary workers have been affected both by temporary and long standing illnesses. Their ailments were found to be related with the chemical and biological hazards they are exposed while doing their sanitation work. A Large number of sanitary workers were found to adopt self medication as the mode of treatment. In order to improve the health conditions of sanitary workers, regular awareness programmes should be conducted to impart knowledge to the workers regarding safety work procedures and usage of personal safety and sanitary materials. The occupational health services can be given to sanitary workers in the form of periodic health monitoring and free inoculation camps.

6

Challenges Faced by the Residents in the Garbage Dumping Area

Salem Corporation has been dumping the garbage in Chettichavadi village. The citizens residing in the nearby areas of the garbage dumping yard have been facing a lot of challenges due to pollution. It affects the health conditions of the residents. The residents of Chettichavadi village complained that the smoke and odour emitted from the garbage yard caused them breathlessness. Since the maximum capacity of inert pits dug was reached and the practice of open dumping of garbage was followed in the dumping yard. It tends to cause more environmental problems as complained by the residents. Though the corporation officials reveal that there was no practice of putting fire on the garbage, it was complained by the residents that there was a practice of setting on fire frequently of solid waste in the dumping yard. The thick black smoke was found to be emitted from the garbage yard, pose severe environmental and health problems. The groundwater sources were also complained to be contaminated, since there is an infiltration of garbage leachate into groundwater. The villagers complained that 65 percent of groundwater in the village was contaminated, which affected the plants and trees in their surroundings. At this outset an attempt was made in this chapter to examine the challenges faced by the residents in the garbage dumping area.

6.1 Health Issues of Households

It is considered that the households in the garbage dumping area would have been affected by health issues. The respondents were asked to state whether any of their family members have been affected by health issues due to the dumping of garbage in their area.

Table 6.1: Demographic Variables and Health Issues of Residents

Demographic Variables	*Groups*	*Frequency*	*Yes*	*No*	*Total*
Gender	Male	No.	134	13	147
		%	91.20%	8.80%	100.00%
	Female	No.	138	15	153
		%	90.20%	9.80%	100.00%
	Total		**272**	**28**	**300**
Age	Less than	No.	5	1	6
	20 years	%	83.30%	16.70%	100.00%
	20 to 40	No.	159	17	176
	years	%	90.30%	9.70%	100.00%
	40 to 60	No.	86	10	96
	years	%	89.60%	10.40%	100.00%
	Above 60	No.	22	0	22
	years	%	100.00%	0.00%	100.00%
	Total		**272**	**28**	**300**
Marital Status	Single	No.	21	1	22
		%	95.50%	4.50%	100.00%
	Married	No.	251	27	278
		%	90.30%	9.70%	100.00%
	Total	**No.**	**272**	**28**	**300**
Size of family	Up to 2	No.	17	2	19
		%	89.50%	10.50%	100.00%
	3 to 4	No.	120	9	129
		%	93.00%	7.00%	100.00%

	5 to 6	No.	101	10	111
		%	91.00%	9.00%	100.00%
	More than 6	No.	34	7	41
		%	82.90%	17.10%	100.00%
	Total	**No.**	**272**	**28**	**300**
Educational Level	School level	No.	120	15	135
		%	88.90%	11.10%	100.00%
	UG level	No.	57	4	61
		%	93.40%	6.60%	100.00%
	PG level	No.	17	0	17
		%	100.00%	0.00%	100.00%
	Others	No.	78	9	87
		%	89.70%	10.30%	100.00%
	Total	**No.**	**272**	**28**	**300**
Occupational Status	Employees	No.	46	8	54
		%	85.20%	14.80%	100.00%
	Business	No.	19	2	21
		%	90.50%	9.50%	100.00%
	Profession	No.	34	1	35
		%	97.10%	2.90%	100.00%
	Housewifes	No.	45	8	53
		%	84.90%	15.10%	100.00%
	Others	No.	128	9	137
		%	93.40%	6.60%	100.00%
	Total	**No.**	**272**	**28**	**300**
Household Monthly Income	Less than Rs. 5000	No.	91	5	96
		%	94.80%	5.20%	100.00%
	Rs.5001 to Rs.10000	No.	99	17	116
		%	85.30%	14.70%	100.00%
	Rs.10001 to Rs.15000	No.	64	4	68
		%	94.10%	5.90%	100.00%
	Above Rs. 15000	No.	18	2	20
		%	90.00%	10.00%	100.00%
	Total	**No.**	**272**	**28**	**300**

Source: Compiled with Primary Data

From the Table 6.1, it could be observed that out of 147 male residents in the garbage dumping area, 91.2 percent of them were affected by health issues and 8.8 percent of them were not affected by any health issues. Roughly equal percentage of male and female were affected by health problems.

Among the 6 residents pertaining to the age group of less than 20 years, 83.3 percent were suffering from health issues while 16.7 percent were not found to be affected by health issues. Out of 176 residents belonging to the age group of 20 to 40 years, 90.3 percent were affected by health issues whereas 9.7 percent were not affected by health issues. Out of 96 residents in the age group of 40 to 60 years, the proportion of residents affected by health issues were found to be 89.6 percent and the proportion of residents not affected by health issues have been ascertained to be 10.4 per cent.

In the case of 22 respondents in the age group of above 60 years, all of them have been found to be affected by health issues. It implies that the residents belonging to the age group of above 60 years were more affected by health issues than any other age group of the residents.

It is evident that out of 22 single residents, the proportion of residents affected by health issues was 95.5 percent and the proportion of residents not affected by health issues were found to be 4.5 per cent. Out of 278 married residents, 90.3 percent of them were affected by health issues while 9.7 percent of them were not affected by health issues. It indicates that single residents were more prone to health issues than the married residents.

The analysis of health issues with reference to the size of family reveals that out of 19 residents belonging to 'up to 2 members' category, 89.5 percent of them were affected by health issues whereas out of 129 residents pertaining to '3 to 4 members' category, 93.0 percent of them were found to be affected by health issues and 7 percent of them were not affected by health issues. It is found that out of 111 residents having family size of 5 to 6 members,

91.0 percent of them were suffering from health issues while 9.0 percent of them did not have health issues. Among 41 residents belonging to the size of family of more than 6 members, 82.9 percent of them were affected by health issues and 17.1 percent of them have reported that they have not been affected by any health issues. It proclaims that the medium size family members (3 to 4 members) were more affected by health issues than other categories of the residents.

The analysis of health issues with reference to the educational level purports that 88.9 percent of the residents with school level education and 93.4 percent of the residents with UG level educational qualification have been affected by health issues whereas 100 percent of the residents with PG level education and 89.7 percent of residents having other levels of education have been subject to health issues.

It indicates that the most affected residents due to garbage dumping were falling under the category of PG level education. Due to their better standard of education, they were aware of the implication of the dumping yard on their health.

It is evinced that out of the 54 salaried employees participated in the survey, 85.2 percent of them have responded that they have been affected by health issues while the proportion of residents engaged in business suffering from health issues were found to be 90.5 per cent. Out of 35 professional residents 97.1 percent of them were reported to be affected by health issues due to garbage dumping in their area. Among 53 housewives 84.9 percent of them have stated that they have been affected by health issues. Out of 137 residents belonging to other forms of employment 93.4 percent have been found to be affected by health issues. Their forms of employment include self employment and daily wage earning works. It denotes that the residents engaged in profession have been affected the most by health issues due to the garbage dumping in their area.

According to the analysis of health issues with reference to the monthly income, out of 96 residents earning a monthly income of less than Rs.5000, the proportion of residents affected by health issues were found to be 94.8 per cent. About 85.3 percent of the residents whose monthly income was Rs.5000 to Rs.10000 stated that they have been suffering from health issues on account of garbage dumping whereas 94.1 percent of the residents earning a monthly income of Rs.10001 to Rs.15000 were affected by health issues. However, it was found that out of 20 residents having a monthly income of more than Rs.15000, the proportion of residents affected by health issues were around 90 per cent. It denotes that high income earners were less affected by health problems, due to their better precaution and protection against diseases.

6.2 Factors affecting the Health Conditions of Households

In order to determine the factors affecting health conditions of households' binary legit regression is used. Where the dependent variable is health conditions of households, which is binary in its nature (1=Affected 2=Not Affected). Independent variables are nature of house, ownership of house, distance between the house and the dumping yard and the longevity of living in the area.

The nature of house had an impact on the health of the household members. Household members in the well constructed houses will have better protection from the pollution emitted from the garbage dumping areas. Thus the present study expected a positive sign to the impact of nature of house on the health of residents in the garbage dumping area. The other variable expected to have positive influence on the health of the residents in the garbage dumping area is the ownership of house. Members of family living in their own houses may have more concern in protecting their environment and surroundings than members from rented houses. The floor of residence plays a significant role in determining the impact of pollution

Table 6.2: Description of Explanatory Categorical Variables

Variable	Type of Variable	Unit of Measurement	Expected Sign
Nature of House	Categorical	1 = Reinforced Concrete Construction 2 = Thatched 3 = Others	+
Ownership of House	Categorical	1 = Own House 2 = Rented House	+
Floor of Residence	Categorical	1 = Ground floor 2 = First floor 3 = Other floors	+
Distance between the House and Dumping Area	Continuous	1=Less than 1 km 2=1 to 2 kms 3=2 to 3 kms 4=More than 3 kms	-
Longevity of living in the area	Continuous	1=Less than 1 year 2=1 to 2 years 3=2 to 3 years 4=More than 3 years	+

emitted from the garbage dumping area. The concentration of traffic related airborne pollutants emitted from vehicles involved in the disposal and dumping of wastes will be more in the ground floor. The distance between the house and dumping yard is also the significant factor in determining the health conditions of households. The less the distance between the house and the dumping yard, more will be the health impact. Thus the present study has assigned negative sign for the relationship between the distance and the garbage dumping area. The longevity of living nearer the garbage dumping area and the health problems are positively related. The longer the living near the garbage dumping area more will be the chance to be affected by diseases.

Table 6.3: Summary of Categorical Variables

Nature of House	RCC	138	46
	Thatched	159	53
	Others	3	1
	Total	300	100
Ownership of House	Own House	253	84
	Rented House	47	16
	Total	300	100
Floor of Residence	Ground floor	146	49
	First floor	129	43
	Other floors	25	8
	Total	300	100
Distance between the House and Dumping Area	1=Less than 1 km	3	1
	2=1 to 2 kms	9	3
	3=2 to 3 kms	48	16
	4=More than 3 kms	240	80
	Total	300	100
Longevity of living in the area	1=Less than 1 year	87	29
	2=1 to 2 years	85	28
	3=2 to 3 years	59	20
	4=More than 3 years	69	23
	Total	300	100

Table 6.4: Omnibus Tests of Model Coefficients

		Chi-square	*Df*	*Sig.*
Step 1	Step	44.868	5	.000
	Block	44.868	5	.000
	Model	44.868	5	.000

The value of chi square and significance of the above model shows that the model has no explanatory power.

Table 6.5: Model Summary

Step	*-2 Log likelihood*	*Cox & Snell R Square*	*Nagelkerke R Square*
1	81.542[a]	.294	.637

The -2 log likelihood statistics of the model is 81.542. Smaller the statistics of -2 log likelihood, better the significance of model. The Cox & Snell R Square statistics is similar to R^2 value in linear regression. The condition for the statistics is that it should not reach the maximum of 1. The Nagelkerke R^2 value can reach the maximum of 1. Based on the conditions, the model fits the data.

Table 6.6: Hosmer and Lemeshow Test

Step	*Chi-square*	*Df*	*Sig.*
1	4.846	8	.774

The insignificant p value suggest that the data fit the model well.

Table 6.7: Variables in the Equation

Variables	B	S.E.	Wald	Df	Sig.	Exp (B)	95% C.I. for EXP(B)	
							Lower	Upper
Distance between the House and Dumping Area	-2.698	.463	33.911	1	.000	.067	.027	.167
Nature of House	-.293	.595	.242	1	.623	.746	.233	2.394
Ownership of House	-1.372	1.005	1.863	1	.172	.254	.035	1.819
Floor of Residence	-.056	.360	.024	1	.877	.946	.467	1.917
Longevity of living in the area	1.719	.422	16.622	1	.000	5.578	2.441	12.746
Constant	3.886	2.474	2.466	1	.116	48.723		

Of the five explanatory variables, two variables viz. longevity of living in the area and the distance between the garbage dumping yard and the houses were significant at one percent. The positive Beta value of longevity of living in the dumping area suggests that more the period of living in the garbage dumping area more will be the chance to be affected by health ailments. The negative Beta value of variable viz. distance between house premises and the garbage dumping area reveals that more the distance less will be the chance to get affected by health problems due to the pollution emitted from the garbage dumping yard.

6.3 Nature of Health Issues Versus Kind, Duration and Expenses of Treatment

For this purpose, the members of the family have been classified as self, spouse, children, parents and others. The nature of health issues has been classified as cold, fever, breathing issues, skin problem, eye sight problems, heart problems and others. The kinds of treatment taken by the citizens have been categorized as medicines only, injection & medicine and surgery. The duration of treatment has been divided into six groups such as less than one week, less than one month, less than 3 months, less than 6 months, less than 1 year and more than 1 year. The expenses spent for treatment have been grouped as less than Rs.1000, Rs.1001 to Rs.2000, Rs.2001 to Rs.5000 and more than Rs.5000.

In this study, an attempt has been made to understand the relationship between the nature of health issues and the kind of treatment, duration of treatment and the treatment expenses of the respondent. In this regard, the following hypotheses have been framed and tested:

Null Hypothesis H_{01}: There is no significant relationship between the nature of health issues and the kind of treatment of the respondents.

Null Hypothesis H_{02}: There is no significant relationship between the nature of health issues and the duration of treatment of the respondents.

Null Hypothesis H_{03}: There is no significant relationship between the nature of health issues and the treatment expenses of the respondents.

Table 6.8: Nature of Health Issues Versus Kind, Duration and Expenses of Treatment of the Respondent

Factor	*Chi square value*	*DF*	*p value*	*Result*
Kind of Treatment	11.63	5	0.040	Rejected *
Duration of Treatment	39.09	20	0.007	Rejected **
Treatment Expenses	22.80	15	0.088	Accepted

* Significant @ 5% ** Significant @ 1%

According to the Table 6.8 the computed value of chi square stating the relationship between the nature of health issues and the kind of treatment of the respondents is 11.63 and the p value is 0.040. Since the p value is less than 0.05, it falls in the rejection region. Hence, the null hypothesis is rejected and it is concluded that there is a significant relationship between the nature of health issues and the kind of treatment of the respondents. It implies that the residents prefer different kinds of treatment for different nature of health issues.

From the analysis, it could be understood that the computed value of chi square indicating the relationship between the nature of health issues and the duration of treatment of the respondent has been 39.09 and the p value is 0.007. Since the p value is less than 0.01, it falls in the rejection region. Hence, the null hypothesis is rejected and it is concluded that there exists a significant relationship between the nature of health issues and the duration of treatment of the respondents. It reveals that the duration of treatment varies significantly for different nature of health issues.

The value of chi square measuring the relationship between the nature of health issues and the treatment expenses of respondents has been computed to be 22.80 while the p value is found to be 0.088. As the p value exceeds 0.05, it falls in the acceptance region. Hence, the null hypothesis is accepted and it is inferred that the relationship between the nature of health issues and the treatment expenses of the respondents is not significant. It denotes that the treatment expenses do not vary significantly in accordance with the nature of health issues.

With a view to understand the relationship between the nature of health issues and the kind of treatment, the duration of treatment and the treatment expenses of the spouse of the respondent the following hypotheses have been framed and tested:

Null Hypothesis H_{01}: There is no significant relationship between the nature of health issues and the kind of treatment of the spouse of the respondents.

Null Hypothesis H_{02}: There is no significant relationship between the nature of health issues and the duration of treatment of the spouse of the respondents.

Null Hypothesis H_{03}: There is no significant relationship between the nature of health issues and the treatment expenses of the spouse of the respondents.

Table 6.9: Nature of Health Issues Versus Kind, Duration and Expenses of Treatment of the Spouse

Factor	*Chi square value*	*DF*	*p value*	*Result*
Kind of Treatment	16.009	10	0.099	Accepted
Duration of Treatment	29.133	20	0.085	Accepted
Treatment Expenses	1m8.903	15	0.218	Accepted

Table 6.9 evinces that the computed value of chi square stating the relationship between the nature of health issues and the kind of treatment of the spouse of respondent is 16.009 and the p value is 0.099. Since the p value is greater than 0.05, it falls in the acceptance region. Hence, the null

hypothesis is accepted and it is concluded that there is no significant relationship between the nature of health issues and the kind of treatment of the spouse. It purports that the residents do not prefer different kinds of treatment for different nature of health issues of the spouse.

From the analysis, it could be understood that the computed value of chi square indicating the relationship between the nature of health issues and the duration of treatment of the spouse has been 29.133 and the p value is 0.085. Since the p value is greater than 0.01, it falls in the acceptance region. Hence, the null hypothesis is accepted and it is concluded that there exists no significant relationship between the nature of health issues and the duration of treatment of the spouse. It reveals that the duration of treatment varies significantly for different nature of health issues of the spouse.

The value of chi square measuring the relationship between the nature of health issues and the treatment expenses of the spouse has been computed to be 18.903 while the p value is found to be 0.218. As the p value exceeds 0.05, it falls in the acceptance region. Hence, the null hypothesis is accepted and it is inferred that the relationship between the nature of health issues and the treatment expenses of the spouse is not significant. It denotes that the treatment expenses do not vary significantly in accordance with the nature of health issues of spouse.

In order to understand the relationship between the nature of health issues and the kind of treatment, the duration of treatment and the treatment expenses of children of the respondents the following hypotheses have been framed and tested:

Null Hypothesis H_{01}: There is no significant relationship between the nature of health issues and the kind of treatment of the children of the respondents.

Null Hypothesis H_{02}: There is no significant relationship between the nature of health issues and the duration of treatment of the children of the respondents.

Null Hypothesis H_{03}: There is no significant relationship between the nature of health issues and the treatment expenses of the children of the respondents.

Table 6.10: Nature of Health Issues Versus Kind, Duration and Expenses of Treatment of the Children

Factor	*Chi square value*	*DF*	*p value*	*Result*
Kind of Treatment	111.962	10	0.000	Rejected **
Duration of Treatment	14.101	15	0.518	Accepted
Treatment Expenses	29.229	15	0.015	Rejected *

* Significant @ 5% ** Significant @ 1%

It is evident from the Table 6.10 that the computed value of chi square stating the relationship between the nature of health issues and the kind of treatment of the children is 111.962 and the p value is 0.000. Since the p value is less than 0.01, it falls in the rejection region. Hence, the null hypothesis is rejected and it is concluded that there is a significant relationship between the nature of health issues and the kind of treatment of the children. It indicates that the residents prefer different kinds of treatment for different nature of health issues of the children.

From the analysis, it could be understood that the computed value of chi square indicating the relationship between the nature of health issues and the duration of treatment of the children has been 14.101 and the p value is 0.518. Since the p value is greater than 0.01, it falls in the acceptance region. Hence, the null hypothesis is accepted and it is concluded that there exists no significant relationship between the nature of health issues and the duration of treatment of the children. It reveals that the duration of treatment varies significantly for different nature of health issues of the children.

The value of chi square measuring the relationship between the nature of health issues and the treatment expenses of children has been computed to be 29.229 while the p value is found to be 0.015. As the p value is less than 0.05, it falls in the rejection region. Hence, the null hypothesis is rejected and it is inferred that the relationship between the nature of health issues and the treatment expenses of the children is significant. It denotes that the treatment expenses vary significantly in accordance with the nature of health issues of the children.

In an attempt to understand the relationship between the nature of health issues and the kind of treatment, the duration of treatment and the treatment expenses of the parents the following hypotheses have been framed and tested:

Null Hypothesis H_{01}: There is no significant relationship between the nature of health issues and the kind of treatment of the parents of the respondents.

Null Hypothesis H_{02}: There is no significant relationship between the nature of health issues and the duration of treatment of the parents of the respondents.

Null Hypothesis H_{03}: There is no significant relationship between the nature of health issues and the treatment expenses of the parents of the respondents.

Table 6.11: Nature of Health Issues Versus Kind, Duration and Expenses of Treatment of the Parents

Factor	*Chi square value*	*DF*	*p value*	*Result*
Kind of Treatment	27.441	10	0.002	Rejected **
Duration of Treatment	26.926	25	0.360	Accepted
Treatment Expenses	24.846	15	0.062	Accepted

From the Table 6.11 it could be observed that the computed value of chi square stating the relationship between the nature of health issues and the kind of treatment of the parents is 27.441 and the p value is 0.002. Since the p value is less than 0.01, it falls in the rejection region. Hence, the null hypothesis is rejected and it is concluded that there is a significant relationship between the nature of health issues and the kind of treatment of the parents. It indicates that the residents prefer different kinds of treatment for different nature of health issues of the parents.

From the analys,s, it could be understood that the computed value of chi square indicating the relationship between the nature of health issues and the duration of treatment of the parents has been 26.926 and the p value is 0.360. Since the p value is greater than 0.01, it falls in the acceptance region. Hence, the null hypothesis is accepted and it is concluded that there exists no significant relationship between the nature of health issues and the duration of treatment of the parents. It reveals that the duration of treatment does not vary significantly for different nature of health issues of the parents.

The value of chi square measuring the relationship between the nature of health issues and the treatment expenses of parents has been computed to be 24.846 while the p value is found to be 0.062. As the p value is greater than 0.05, it falls in the acceptance region. Hence, the null hypothesis is accepted and it is inferred that the relationship between the nature of health issues and the treatment expenses of parents is not significant. It denotes that the treatment expenses do not vary significantly in accordance with the nature of health issues of the parents.

With a view to understand the relationship between the nature of health issues and the kind of treatment, the duration of treatment and the treatment expenses of other members of the family the following hypotheses have been framed and tested:

Null Hypothesis H_{01}: There is no significant relationship between the nature of health issues and the kind of treatment of other members of the family.

Null Hypothesis H_{02}: There is no significant relationship between the nature of health issues and the duration of treatment of other members of the family.

Null Hypothesis H_{03}: There is no significant relationship between the nature of health issues and the treatment expenses of other members of the family.

Table 6.12: Nature of Health Issues Versus Kind, Duration and Expenses of Treatment of other Family Members

Factor	*Chi square value*	*DF*	*p value*	*Result*
Kind of Treatment	27.283	10	0.002	Rejected **
Duration of Treatment	37.761	20	0.009	Rejected **
Treatment Expenses	20.817	15	0.143	Accepted

Source: Compiled with Primary Data

According to the Table 6.12 the computed value of chi square stating the relationship between the nature of health issues and the kind of treatment of other members of the family is 27.283 and the p value is 0.002. Since the p value is less than 0.01, it falls in the rejection region. Hence, the null hypothesis is rejected and it is concluded that there is a significant relationship between the nature of health issues and the kind of treatment of other members of the family. It indicates that the residents prefer different kinds of treatment for different nature of health issues of other members of the family.

From the analysis, it could be understood that the computed value of chi square indicating the relationship between the nature of health issues and the duration of treatment of other members of the family has been 37.761 and the p value is 0.009. Since the p value is less than 0.01, it falls in the rejection region. Hence, the null hypothesis is rejected and it is concluded that there exists a significant relationship between the nature of health issues and the duration of treatment of other members of the family. It reveals that the duration of treatment varies significantly for different nature of health issues of other members of the family.

The value of chi square measuring the relationship between the nature of health issues and treatment expenses of other members of the family has been computed to be 20.817 while the p value is found to be 0.143. As the p value is greater than 0.05, it falls in the acceptance region.

Hence, the null hypothesis is accepted and it is inferred that the relationship between the nature of health issues and the treatment expenses of other members of the family is not significant. It denotes that the treatment expenses do not vary significantly in accordance with the nature of health issues of other members of the family.

6.4 Perception on Garbage Dumping

In order to fulfil the objectives of the study, the citizens residing in the garbage dumping area have been asked to state their level of agreement to the following statements regarding their perception on garbage dumping:

1. Garbage dumping has caused air pollution in our area.
2. Garbage dumping has caused water pollution in our area.
3. Environment is affected due to garbage dumping.
4. Bad smell disturbs the people.
5. When the solid waste is burnt smoke creates disturbances.
6. Children are unable to play on the roads.
7. Aged people are suffering from eye irritation.
8. Corporation vehicles carrying the solid waste create traffic issues.
9. Garbage is not properly dumped.
10. No proper method is followed for the solid waste management.

The level of agreement has been obtained from the respondents in a five-point scale and the scores have been assigned as to 5 for Strongly Agree; 4 for Agree; 3 for Neutral; 2 for Disagree; and 1 for Strongly Disagree.

The scores assigned to each of these ten statements have been summed up and the total scores have been taken for the analysis. The relationship between demographic variables and perception on garbage dumping has been analyzed in this study.

Age and Perception on Garbage Dumping

With a view to understand the relationship between the age of the respondents and their perception on garbage dumping, the following hypotheses have been framed and tested:

Null Hypothesis H_0: There is no significant relationship between the age of the respondents and their perception on garbage dumping.

Alternative Hypothesis H_1: There is a significant relationship between the age of the respondents and their perception n garbage dumping.

Table 6.13: Age and Perception on Garbage Dumping- Anova

Source of variation	*Sum of Squares*	*DF*	*Mean Square*	*F value*	*p value*	*Result*
Between Groups	27.266	3	9.089	0.356	0.785	Accepted
Within Groups	7550.734	296	25.509			
Total	7578	299				

Table 6.13 reveals that the F value measuring the relationship between the age of the respondents and their perception on garbage dumping has been found to be 0.356 while the p value is 0.785. Since the p value is greater than 0.05, it falls in the acceptance region. Hence, the null hypothesis is accepted. The hypothesis that 'there is no significant relationship between the age of the respondents and their perception on garbage dumping' holds good. It is inferred that the perception of respondents on garbage dumping does not vary significantly in accordance with their age. The respondents from all age groups both younger and older were equally aware of the hazards of the dumping area. The respondents from younger and middle age group due their better level of education and exposure were aware of the environmental implications of dumping area situated in their village. Similarly respondents of older age groups due to their better

experience and longevity of living in the area were equally aware of the environmental impact of dumping of wastes in their village.

Gender and Perception on Garbage Dumping

With a view to understand the relationship between the gender of the respondents and their perception on garbage dumping the following hypotheses have been framed and tested:

Null Hypothesis H_0: There is no significant relationship between the gender of the respondents and their perception on garbage dumping.

Alternative Hypothesis H_1: There is a significant relationship between the gender of the respondents and their perception on garbage dumping.

Table 6.14: Gender and Perception on Garbage Dumping – Anova

Total Score	*Sum of Squares*	*DF*	*Mean Square*	*F*	*Significant*
Between Groups	32.288	1	32.288	1.275	.260
Within Groups	7545.712	298	25.321		
Total	7578.000	299			

According to the Table 6.14, the F value measuring the relationship between the gender of the respondents and their perception on garbage dumping has been found to be 1.275 while the p value is 0.26. Since the p value is greater than 0.05, it falls in the acceptance region. Hence, the null hypothesis is accepted. The hypothesis that 'there is no significant relationship between the gender of the respondents and their perception on garbage dumping' holds good. It is inferred that the perception of respondents on garbage dumping does not vary significantly in accordance with their gender. Both male and female gender was equally aware of the pollution caused by the dumping area.

Marital Status and Perception on Garbage Dumping

With a view to understand the relationship between the marital status of the respondents and their perception on garbage dumping the following hypotheses have been framed and tested:

Null Hypothesis H_0: There is no significant relationship between the marital status of the respondents and their perception on garbage dumping.

Alternative Hypothesis H_1: There is a significant relationship between the marital status of the respondents and their perception on garbage dumping.

Table 6.15: Marital Status and Perception on Garbage Dumping - Anova

Total Score	*Sum of Squares*	*DF*	*Mean Square*	*F*	*Significant*
Between Groups	293.654	1	293.654	4.611	.033
Within Groups	18977.292	298	63.682		
Total	**19270.947**	**299**			

Table 6.15 purports the F value measuring the relationship between the marital status of the respondents and their perception on garbage dumping has been found to be 4.611 while the p value is 0.033. Since the p value is less than 0.05, it falls in the rejection region. Hence, the null hypothesis is rejected. The hypothesis that 'there is a significant relationship between the marital status of the respondents and their perception on garbage dumping' holds good. It is inferred that the perception of respondents on the garbage dumping vary significantly in accordance with their marital status. It implies that the married respondents have better level awareness of the environmental implications of dumping of wastes in their area than the unmarried respondents.

Size of Family and Perception on Garbage Dumping

With a view to understand the relationship between the size of family of the respondents and their perception on garbage dumping the following hypotheses have been framed and tested:

Null Hypothesis H_0: There is no significant relationship between the size of family of the respondents and their perception on garbage dumping.

Alternative Hypothesis H_1: There is a significant relationship between the size of family of the respondents and their perception on garbage dumping.

Table 6.16: Size of Family and Perception on Garbage Dumping – Anova

Source of variation	*Sum of Squares*	*DF*	*Mean Square*	*F value*	*p value*	*Result*
Between Groups	340.387	3	113.462	4.64	0.003	Rejected**
Within Groups	7237.613	296	24.451			
Total	**7578**	**299**				

It is evinced from the Table 6.16 that the F value measuring the relationship between the size of family of the respondents and their perception on garbage dumping has been found to be 4.64 while the p value is 0.003. Since the p value is less than 0.01, it falls in the rejection region. Hence, the null hypothesis is rejected and the alternative hypothesis is accepted. The hypothesis that 'there is a significant relationship between the size of family of the respondents and their perception on garbage dumping' holds good. It is inferred that the perception of respondents on the garbage dumping vary significantly in accordance with the size of the family. The household having more number of members is able to obtain the experience and awareness about the environmental conditions of their surroundings from their elder and younger members than small sized households.

Educational Level and Perception on Garbage Dumping

With a view to understand the relationship between educational level of the respondents and their perception on garbage dumping the following hypotheses have been framed and tested:

Null Hypothesis H_0: There is no significant relationship between the educational level of the respondents and their perception on garbage dumping.

Alternative Hypothesis H_1: There is a significant relationship between the educational level of the respondents and their perception on garbage dumping.

Table 6.17: Educational Level and Perception on Garbage Dumping - Anova

Source of variation	*Sum of Squares*	*DF*	*Mean Square*	*F value*	*p value*	*Result*
Between Groups	992.839	3	330.946	5.382	0.001	Accepted
Within Groups	18200.948	296	61.490			
Total	19193.787	299				

According to the Table 6.17, the F value measuring the relationship between the educational level of the respondents and their perception on garbage dumping has been found to be while the p value is 0.001. Since the p value is less than 0.05, it falls in the acceptance region. Hence, the null hypothesis is rejected. The hypothesis that 'there is a significant relationship between the educational level of the respondents and their perception on garbage dumping' holds good. It is inferred that the perception of respondents on garbage dumping vary significantly in accordance with their educational level. The sample respondents with the higher educational qualification were more aware of the ill effects of the garbage dumping yard than the uneducated respondents.

Occupational Status and Perception on Garbage Dumping

With a view to understand the relationship between the occupational status of the respondents and their perception on garbage dumping the following hypotheses have been framed and tested:

Null Hypothesis H_0: There is no significant relationship between the occupational status of the respondents and their perception on garbage dumping.

Alternative Hypothesis H_1: There is a significant relationship between the occupational status of the respondents and their perception on garbage dumping.

Table 6.18: Occupational Status and Perception on Garbage Dumping – Anova

Source of variation	*Sum of Squares*	*DF*	*Mean Square*	*F value*	*p value*	*Result*
Between Groups	184.644	4	46.161	1.842	0.121	Accepted
Within Groups	7393.356	295	25.062			
Total	7578	299				

Table 6.18 envisages that the F value measuring the relationship between the occupational status of the respondents and their perception on garbage dumping has been found to be 1.842 while the p value is 0.121. Since the p value is greater than 0.05, it falls in the acceptance region. Hence, the null hypothesis is accepted. The hypothesis that 'there is no significant relationship between the occupational status of the respondents and their perception on garbage dumping' holds good. It is inferred that the perception of respondents on garbage dumping does not vary significantly in accordance with their occupational status.

Monthly Income and Perception on Garbage Dumping

With a view to understand the relationship between the monthly income of the respondents and their perception on garbage dumping the following hypotheses have been framed and tested:

Null Hypothesis H_0: There is no significant relationship between the monthly income of the respondents and their perception on garbage dumping.

Alternative Hypothesis H_1: There is a significant relationship between the monthly income of the respondents and their perception on garbage dumping.

Table 6.19: Monthly Income and Perception on Garbage Dumping - Anova

Source of variation	*Sum of Squares*	*DF*	*Mean Square*	*F value*	*p value*	*Result*
Between Groups	520.834	3	173.611	7.282	0.000	Rejected **
Within Groups	7057.166	296	23.842			
Total	7578	299				

According to the Table 6.19, the F value measuring the relationship between the monthly income of the respondents and their perception on garbage dumping has been found to be 7.282 while the p value is 0.000. Since the p value is less than 0.01, it falls in the rejection region. Hence, the null hypothesis is rejected and the alternative hypothesis is accepted. The hypothesis that 'there is a significant relationship between the monthly income of the respondents and their perception on garbage dumping' holds good. It is inferred that the perception of respondents on garbage dumping varies significantly in accordance with their monthly income. It can be interpreted that the category of higher income group has more awareness due to their better level of education about the environmental problems of dumping area in their village.

From the forgoing analysis on the impact of the garbage dumping yard, on the residents in Chettichavadi village, where the dumping yard is located, it is inferred that the health of the residents living nearer to the garbage dumping yard were more affected. The other major factors determining the health conditions of the residents is the longevity of their living in the village, where the dumping yard is situated. The major health ailments revealed by the households of Chettichavadi village were allergy, breathing problems, eye irritation and viral infections. The flies, odour and smoke from the garbage dumping yard were found to cause health ailments to the households. Daily 350 to 400 tonnes of waste from Salem Corporation were dumped at the village.

The practice of dumping of waste is done in the village for several years. The Lorries and tractors transporting the waste to the dumping yard are also huge in number in the village. Regarding the level of perception and awareness about the dumping of waste in their village, the residents were more aware of the hazards of the garbage dumping yard. Thus it is the role of the Corporation to adopt scientific methods of disposal and management of waste to avoid mere dumping of waste in Chettichavadi village.

7

Findings, Suggestions and Conclusion

The present study has been undertaken with the main objective of analyzing the economics of municipal solid waste management in Salem Corporation. For the purpose of this study, six objectives have been framed. The objectives of the study include examining the quantum of solid waste its disposal methods, analyzing the health concerns of sanitary workers, measuring the willingness to pay of the public for better management of solid waste, identifying the challenges faced by the residents in the garbage dumping area, assessing the efficiency of Salem Corporation in solid waste management and offering suggestions for improving the solid waste management. The primary data analyses have been made in three chapters. The fourth chapter discussed the quantum of solid waste, its disposal methods, efficiency of waste management and willingness to pay by households for improved solid waste management, while the fifth chapter described the analysis regarding health concerns of sanitary workers and the sixth chapter dealt with the challenges faced by the residents in the garbage dumping area. The major findings have been summarized in this chapter.

7.1 Major Findings of the Study

The following are the major findings of the study:

The analysis of solid waste generated in the four zones of Salem Corporation revealed that the highest quantity of solid waste has been generated in the Hasthampatti zone followed by Suramangalam zone and Kondalampatti zone while the lowest solid waste generating zone is the Ammapet zone. It is understood that the solid waste generated varied significantly from one zone to another.

It is observed from the analysis of relationship between monthly income and solid waste generated that high income group earning monthly income more than Rs.20000 has been the highest solid waste generating group among the different monthly income earning groups. The lowest solid waste has been generated by the low income group whose monthly income is less than Rs.5000. It implies that the solid waste generation increases as the monthly income increases.

The results indicated that the households headed by respondents who have completed post graduation and above have been the highest solid waste generating group while the households headed by illiterates have been the lowest solid waste generating group among the sample households. It denotes that the larger quantity of solid waste has been generated by the highly educated group of respondents. The significant difference was found in the quantity of waste generated between the different educational standards of the household heads.

Occupation plays a significant role in determining the quantity of waste generated by them. The larger amount of solid waste has been generated by the households headed by respondents occupied in business than other categories. The households headed by respondents occupied as coolies have been found to be the lowest waste generating group.

The variables viz. households' income, family size, educational qualification and personal attitude were significant in determining the total waste generated by the households.

Disposing the waste in municipal waste bins was the method of disposal largely followed in Salem Corporation followed by discharging at road sides, canals etc. No significant difference was found in the methods of disposal of solid waste followed by households among the four zones in Salem Corporation.

Majority of sample households failed to sort and separate their waste before disposal. It implies that sorting and separating before disposal did not vary among the households of the four zones of Salem Corporation.

Around half of the households reveal that there was a daily clearance of waste in their area followed by clearance at once in three days. No significant difference is observed in the frequency of clearance of solid waste among the households of the four zones of Salem Corporation.

Of the 385 sample households roughly equal number of households assessed that the performance of solid waste management by Salem Corporation was good. There is a significant difference in the performance of Salem Corporation in solid waste management among the four zones of Salem Corporation as indicated by the households.

Tricycles were the major mode of collection and disposal of solid wastes in Salem Corporation, which was largely used in Hasthampatti Zone followed by Suramangalam Zone. The significant difference was found in the methods of collection and disposal of solid waste among four zones.

The majority households were largely affected by signs and symptoms and the remaining were largely affected by diseases. Among the category of households largely affected by signs and symptoms larger percent were found in Suramangalam Zone. Majority of households in Ammapet Zone, were found to be affected by diseases largely. A significant difference was found in the signs and symptoms and diseases among four zones.

The factors viz. quantity of waste generated, frequency of waste collection and disposal and perception about the waste management of the Corporation in their area were found significant in determining the impact of improper solid waste management on health ailments. The attitude of household head towards segregation and reuse of solid waste is insignificant in determining the impact of improper solid waste management on health of household members.

Among the 385 households considered for the study, the majority were not willing to pay for improved solid waste management.

The factors viz. age, gender, perception towards environment, family income and ownership of house were found to be significant in determining the willingness to pay for the improved solid waste management. The other factors viz. quantity of waste generation, attitude towards segregation and separation of solid waste, size of family and educational qualification were insignificant in determining the willingness to pay.

The amount of willingness to pay for better management of solid waste did not vary significantly according to the zones. Households in all zones are equally willing to pay for improved solid waste management.

A significant relationship was found between income, education and occupation and the amount of willing to pay extra cost for disposal and management of solid waste.

The major reasons attributed for the amount of willing to pay extra for solid waste management were improvement in health conditions and better environmental management. No significant difference was found in the reasons attributed for the willingness to pay for solid waste management among the four zones.

7.2 Analysis of Health Conditions of Sanitary Workers

Of the 193 sanitary workers, majority i.e. 89.64 per cent have been affected by any one of occupational ailments viz. skin problems, occupational injuries, chest pain, respiratory infections, eye problems, bacterial, viral and fungal infections and musculoskeletal disorders. They have been affected both by temporary and chronic illnesses.

No significant relationship was found between age, gender, education, income and nature of work of sanitary workers and the level of their agreement to injury while performing their sanitary work.

Except age, all other factors viz., gender, education, income and nature of work were found to have insignificant relationship with the level of agreement of sanitary workers towards the suffering from temporary illnesses due to sanitary work.

No significant relationship was found between age, gender, education, income and nature of work of sanitary workers and the level of their agreement towards suffering from acute illness due to sanitary work.

The level of education and income of the sanitary workers were found to have significant relationship with their level of agreement towards getting treatment from government hospitals for their ailment.

Gender is the only factor found significantly related with the level of agreement towards starting their sanitary work in the very early morning. Educational standard of sanitary workers is found significantly related with their level of agreement that they have been given excessive workload.

Though all the sanitary workers were provided sanitary materials, majority (86.52 per cent) failed to use those materials due to their discomfort in using those materials and unawareness about its usage.

Regarding the occupational health hazards there exists no significant difference among the sanitary workers engaged in different nature of work viz. sweeping, collection, loading and disposal of waste. It implies that all types of sanitation work were equally infectious in causing ailments unless safeguarded with sanitary equipments.

A significant difference is observed between the medical expenses incurred by the sanitary workers affected by occupational health hazards and those who were unaffected. The sanitary workers facing occupational health hazards were found to incur large amount of medical expenses when compared to others.

Regarding the methods of medical treatment preferred, around 49.7 per cent mostly prefer allopathic medicine for their treatment both from Government and private hospitals.

7.3 Analysis of Problems faced by Households Residing near Dumping Area

The analysis of nature of health problems faced by the residents of dumping area denotes that longevity of living has significantly influenced the nature of health issues faced by them.

It could be understood that nature of house, ownership of house and the floor of residence have no significant impact on the health issue faced by the residents of dumping area while distance between the house and dumping area and longevity of living in the area have made significant impact on the health hazards faced by them.

The results indicate that kind of treatment and duration of treatment vary significantly according to the nature of health issues while treatment expenses is not significantly influenced by the nature of health issues of respondents residing in dumping areas. On the other hand the nature of health issues of spouse of the respondent has no significant relationship with kind of treatment, duration of treatment and treatment expenses.

The duration of treatment did not vary significantly in accordance with the nature of health issues faced by the children of the respondents. However, there is a significant variation in the kind of treatment and treatment expenses according to the nature of health issues faced by the children of respondents.

There is strong evidence that the kind of treatment varied significantly in accordance with the nature of health issues faced by the parents of the respondents. On the other hand, no significant variation is found in the duration of treatment and treatment expenses on account of nature of health issues faced by the parents of the sanitary workers.

It is realized from the analysis that the kind of treatment and duration of treatment varied significantly in accordance with the nature of health issues faced by other family members of respondents. However, treatment expenses have no significant relationship with the nature of health issues faced by other family members.

The analysis of perception of residents towards garbage dumping reveals that there is no significant relationship between age of the residents and their perception towards garbage dumping. The perception of the residents towards garbage dumping did not vary significantly according to their gender. The perception of respondents on garbage dumping varies significantly in accordance with their marital status.

The perception of respondents on garbage dumping varies significantly in accordance with their educational level. The sample respondents with higher educational qualification were more aware of ill effects of dumping yard than uneducated respondents. The perception of respondents on garbage dumping does not vary significantly in accordance with their occupational status. The perception of respondents on garbage dumping varies significantly in accordance with their monthly income. It can be interpreted that the category of higher income group has more awareness due to their better level of education about the environmental problems of dumping area in their village.

7.4 Suggestions

The key findings of the study entitled, "Economics of Municipal Solid Waste Management in Salem Corporation" as presented above revealed many facts about the performance of Salem Corporation towards Solid Waste

Management. On the basis of the research findings, the following suggestions have been offered for improving the Solid Waste Management of Salem Corporation:

It is suggested that the households in Salem corporation shall be encouraged to reduce their quantity solid waste generation by inculcating wealth out of waste programmes among them.

The households earning higher income should be imposed local tax on the higher amount of solid waste generated by them.

Being the most widely used method of disposal, it is suggested that municipal waste bin shall be provided in all the areas of Salem Corporation.

Awareness and training campaign shall be conducted to the citizens of Salem Corporation to realize the significance of sorting and separating the solid waste before disposal and accordingly they shall be motivated to sort and separate the solid waste before disposal.

Daily clearance of solid waste shall be insisted to be followed in all the areas of the Salem Corporation which would help avoiding the health hazards.

Decentralized system of segregation and collection of waste involving the role of public, NGOs and self help groups should be introduced to improve the efficiency in waste management.

The rag pickers can be officially employed to enable the better segregation and collection of wastes.

Tricycle is the most widely used vehicle for collection of domestic garbage. Hence, sanitary workers are to be provided tricycles in different sizes according to the quantity of waste collected by them.

In the event of necessity, the citizens shall be encouraged to pay extra cost for disposal of solid waste. It would enable the municipal authorities to control the expenses and improve the performance of solid waste management of the corporation.

First aid kits shall be provided to the sanitary workers at the duty allocation centres with a view to manage their temporary illnesses due to the sanitary work.

Separate wards shall be provided in primary health centres and Government hospitals for sanitary workers in order to provide better and faster treatment to them.

The time schedule for sanitary work shall be fixed to avoid excessive work load given to them.

Sanitary workers should be sensitized to properly use sanitary materials in order to minimize their occupational health hazards.

To improve the health conditions of sanitary workers, regular awareness programmes should be conducted to impart knowledge to the workers regarding safety work procedures and hygiene practices.

The occupational health services should be given to sanitary workers in the form of periodic health monitoring and free inoculation camps.

Since there is a significant relationship between longevity of living and distance between residence and dumping yard and nature of health issue faced by the residents, it is better to identify the dumping yard in a faraway place away from residential area.

It is also suggested that the number of garbage dumping yards shall be increased in order to minimize the quantum of garbage dumped in a particular yard.

In order to avoid mere dumping of solid waste, new technology shall be invented to scientifically manage the solid waste without emitting the smoke.

The garbage dumped in the yards shall be disposed off immediately at regular intervals to avoid its environmental implications.

Since there is a possibility of getting a positive externality from solid wastes, if it is properly managed by obtaining byproducts viz. biogas, compost and recyclable plastics which have monetary value, it should be attempted by the Corporation.

7.5 Conclusion

The solid waste management was found as the serious environmental challenge faced by Salem Corporation. So far no scientific method of management was followed in the Corporation. Though it was attempted through the mode of public private participation at Chettichavadi Village a few years ago, it was stopped due to many technical constraints. From the primary data analysis collected from households, it was found that due to the improper management of solid waste, they were prone to serious health problems. The residents at Chettichavadi village, where the entire waste collected from the Corporation premises were dumped, were found affected by many health ailments. It shows the failure of the Corporation in managing and treating their waste in a scientific manner. The ban of throwaway plastics and the initiation to install modern bio-methanation plants to treat solid waste were found to somehow reduce the volume waste and improve the management of solid waste in the study area. The inclusion of all stakeholders' viz. municipal authorities, NGOs, waste collectors, waste processers, waste generators, research institutes, academics, media and environmental regulators should be undertaken to manage the solid waste in a systematic and viable manner.

Scope for Further Research

It is suggested that further researches shall be carried out to compare and contrast the performance of several Municipal Corporations in Solid Waste Management. The studies analyzing the effectiveness of different methods of management of solid waste shall be conducted. It is also suggested that further studies shall be carried out on the effectiveness of 'Clean India' Project.

Bibliography

1. Achillas et al., (2011), "Social Acceptance for the Development of Waste to Energy Plant in an Urban area", *Resources, Conservation and Recycling,* Vol.55, No.9 - 10, pp 857 - 863.
2. Almitra H. Patel, (2006), *The Hindu,* Tuesday, August 22.
3. Amina Zia et al., (2017), "Influence of Income Level and Seasons on Quantity and Composition of Municipal Solid Waste - A Case Study of Capital City of Pakistan", *Journal of Sustainability,* Vol.9, available at http://www.mdpi.com.
4. Anne Scheinberg et al., (2010), "Solid Waste Management in the World's Cities, UN – HABITAT", *Waste Management and Research,* Vol. 30, No.3, pp. 1 - 16.
5. Anurit Kanti, (2018), "5 Best Waste Management Practices and Innovations Across the Globe", available at http://www.businessworld.com.
6. Asare W et al., (2015), "Household Solid Waste Generation and Disposal in some Selected Communities in Ejisu - Juaben Municipality, Ghana", *Journal of Scientific Research and Reports,* Vol. 6, No.5, pp. 371 - 382.
7. Barnett A.H and Bruce Yandle, (1999), " The End of Externality Revolution" available at http://www.mises.org/
8. Bhatt M S and Asheref Illiyan (2012), "*Solid Waste Management in Indian Perspective*", Synergy Books India, New Delhi.
9. Bhide A.D. and B.B. Sundaresan (2001), "*Solid Waste Management - Collection, Processing and Disposal*", Mudrashllpa Offset Printers, Nagpur.
10. Bijan Maskey and Mrinila Singh (2017), "Households' Willingness to Pay for Improved Waste Collection Service

in Gorkha Municipality of Nepal", *Journal of Environments*, available at https://www.mdpi.com/.

11. Brain P. Simpson, (2007), "An Economic, Political and Philosophical Analysis of Externalities", available at http://www.reasonpapers.com.
12. Chabra, (2003), "Management options of Municipal Solid Waste of Indian Cities", In *Management of Environmental Pollution*, Anju Kohli, Sadhana Kothari and A.P. Chaudhary (eds), in Book Enclave, Jaipur, pp 160 - 169.
13. Chandrappa, Ramesha et al., (2012), *Solid Waste Management Principles and Practices*, Springer Publishing Company, New York.
14. Charles D. Kolstad, (1996), "Uncertainity, Learning, Stock Externalities and Capital Irreversibilities, *Journal of Public Economics*, Vol. 60, No. 2, available at http://www.sciencedirect.com.
15. Christine Furedy, (2002), " Urban Waste and Rural Farmers: Enabling Low Cost Organic Waste Refuse in Developing Countries" available at online http://www.city farmers.org/urbanruralwaste.html
16. Coase R H, (1960), "The Problem of Social Cost", *The Journal of Law and Economics*, Vol.3, available at https://www/jstor.org/.
17. Ezekiel N. Nadunda and Virginia K.Muia (2018), "Estimating the Willingness to pay for improved Municipal solid Waste Management in Nairobi, Kenya", *International journal of Environmental Science*, Vol.3, pp 8 - 16. available at http://www.iaras.org/iaras/journals/ijes
18. Gopalakrishnan K, (2001), "Improved Optimal System for Collection and Transportation of Urban Waste", In *Environmental Pollution and Protection*, M.R. Garg, V.K. Bansal and N.S. Tiwana, (eds), Deep and Deep Publications Private Ltd, Delhi, pp 210 - 220.
19. Igwe Kelechi Chima, Mgbasonwu Vincent Nwabinye (2017), "Economic analysis of Household Waste Generation, Disposal and Management in Umuahia Metropolis, Abia State, Nigeria", *Health Economics and policy*, Vol.2, No.2, pp 47 - 56. available at http://www.sciencepublishinggroup.com.
20. Isaac Bright Addo and Emmanuel Opoku Acheampong, (2015), "Solid Waste Management and its Health Implications on the Dwellers of Kumasi Metropolis, Ghana", *Current*

Research Journal of Social Sciences, Vol.7, No. 3, pp 81 - 93.

21. Jain A.K, (2005), "Municipal Solid Waste Management and Certain Facts, on Environment Protection included in Hindu Religion", *Our Earth,* Vol.2, No.2, June 2005, p. 9.
22. Kannal Achuthan et al., (2007), "Chennai is Running Short of Dumping Space", *The Hindu,* 06.02.2007.
23. Kim Peters, (2001), "Community based Waste Management for Environmental Management and Income Generation in Low Income Areas: A case study of Nairobi Kenya", available at http://www..cityfarmers.org/ nairobibicompost.html
24. Koushki P.A, et al., (2004), "Collection and Transportation Cost of Household Solid Waste in Kuwait", *Journal of Waste Management*, Vol.24, No.9, pp. 957–964.
25. Mansoor Alam Siddiqe, (2000), *Urban Impact of Fringe Areas,* B.R. Publishing Corporation, New Delhi.
26. Medina M, (1997), "Effect of Income on Municipal Solid Waste Generation Rates for Countries of Varying Levels of Economic Development: A Model", *Journal of Solid Waste Technology and Management*, Vol.24, No.3, pp. 149-155.
27. Misra V and Pandey S, (2005), "Hazardous Waste, Impact on Health and Environment Strategies in future in India", *International Journal of Environment*, Vol.31, No.3, pp. 417-431.
28. Mohd. Dinie Muhaimin Samsudina, Mashitah Mat Don, (2012), "Municipal Solid Waste Management in Malaysia: Current Practices, Challenges and Prospects", *Journal of Teknologi*, Vol.62, No.1, pp 95 - 101.
29. Muhdin Muhammedhussen Batu, Ermyas Admasu and Fikadu Tolosa (2016), "Determinants of Households' Willingness to pay for improved Solid Waste Management in Ethiopia: The case study of Jimma Town", *Journal of Environment and Earth Science*, Vol.6, No.7, pp 64 – 77.
30. Nadi Behzad ed al., (2011), "Challenges of Solid Waste Management in Malaysia", *Research Journal of Chemistry and Environment*, Vol.15, No.2, pp. 597-600.
31. Ng and Yang, (1993), "Effects of externality - corrective taxation on the extent of the Market and network size of division of labour", available at http://www.ssrn.com.
32. Nilanthi J G J Bandara, J. Patrick A. Hettiaratchi, S. C. Wirasinghe (2007), "Relation of Waste Generation and

Composition to Socio-Economic Factors: A Case Study", *Journal of Environmental Monitoring and Assessment*, Vol. 135, pp. 31-39.

33. Noorjahan Arif & M. Ravichandran (2011), *Environmental Management - Clean Development Mechanism for Solid Waste: Environmental Economics*, Lambert Academic Publishing, Germany.

34. Ojok J. et al., (2012), "Households Willingness to pay for Improved Municipal Solid Waste Management Services in Kampala, Uganda", *Science Journal of Environmental Engineering Research*, Vol.20, No.12, pp. 1–8.

35. Pervez Alam and K.Ahmade, (2013), "Impact of Solid Waste Management on Health and the Environment", *International Journal of Sustainable Development and Green Economics*, Vol. 2, No.11, pp 165-168.

36. Pham Thi Thuy Trang et al., (2016), "The Effects of Socio-Economic Factors on Household Solid Waste Generation and Composition: A Case Study in Thu Dau Mot, Vietnam", *Journal of Energy Procedia*, Vol. 107, pp 253 - 258, available at http://www.sciencedirect.com

37. Pham Thi Thuy Trang, Dinh Quang Toan and Nguyen Thi Xuan Hanh (2017), "Estimating Household Willingness to pay for improved Solid Waste Management: A Case Study of Thu Dau Mot City, Binh Duong", MATEC Web of Conferences 95, 18004 (2017) ICMME 2016 , pp 1 - 4 available at http://www.creativecommons.org/licenses/by /4.0/

38. Priyanka V. Patil and R. K. Kamble, (2017), "Occupational Health Hazards in Sanitary Workers of Chandrapur City, Central India", *International journal of Environment*, Vol 6, No 3 , pp 15 – 24.

39. Qingbin Song A.B, Zhishi Wang A, and Jinhui Li B, (2016), "Residents Attitudes and Willingness to pay for Solid Waste Management in Macau", *Journal of Procedia Environmental Sciences*, Vol.31, pp 635 - 643.

40. Rafia Afroz, Keisuke Hanaki and Rabaah Tudin, (2010), "Factors Affecting Waste Generation: A Study in a Waste Management Program in Dhaka City, Bangladesh", *Journal of Environmental Monitoring and Assessment*, Vol.179, No. 4, pp 509 - 519.

41. Rajnarayan R. Tiwari, (2012), "Occupational Health Hazards in Sewage and Sanitary Workers", *Indian Journal of Occupational*